THE PSYCHIC
CASE FILES

Also by Tony Stockwell

Spirited

Embracing Eternity

THE PSYCHIC CASE FILES

TONY STOCKWELL

HODDER &
STOUGHTON

First published in Great Britain by Hodder & Stoughton
A division of Hodder Headline

The right of Tony Stockwell to be identified as the Author of the Work
has been asserted by him in accordance with the Copyright,
Designs and Patents Act 1988.

A Hodder & Stoughton Book

1

A CIP catalogue record for this title is available from the British Library

ISBN 978 0340 935637

Typeset in Minion by Hewer Text UK Ltd, Edinburgh

Printed and bound by Mackays of Chatham Ltd, Chatham, Kent

Hodder Headline's policy is to use papers that are natural, renewable
and recyclable products and made from wood grown in sustainable forests.
The logging and manufacturing processes are expected to conform to the
environmental regulations of the country of origin.

For Hilary and Craig Goldman
for believing in me

CONTENTS

INTRODUCTION: Silent Witnesses

In the real world, police or relatives investigating a murder or mysterious death can't conveniently chat with the victim's ghost as they can in plays, novels or movies, but it's important to point out that crimes and mysteries are not always solved by conventional investigative work. It's well known that the process of unravelling a mystery isn't just about painstaking detail, hours of hard work and patience and sophisticated techniques – such as DNA testing, psychological profiling and computerised data analysis – but also about professional wisdom, experience, luck, hunches and, more often than not, gut instinct. What is less well known is that sometimes the police, investigators or relatives desperately searching for information about the fate of a lost loved one, have received vital information or leads from psychics – psychics like me.

MY STORY

I categorise myself as a psychic medium – someone who is able to sense and feel not only energies that emanate from my surroundings and other people but spirits from the other world – and I have two spirit guides, Zintar and Star, who help bring me messages from the other world. They are very much my unseen friends, choosing only to show themselves when needed, and over the years I have grown to love them and regard them as part of my family. Zintar shows himself as an elderly man, wise and gentle. Star on the other hand has never allowed me to see him directly and I experience him as a being of pure white light, often standing to my left.

I was born in the East End of London in 1969. During my very early childhood I was much the same as any other boy but looking back I realise now that the spirit world was very much a part of my childhood from about the age of four. I recall playing alone for hours, quite content to watch the spirit lights that would float around my room, all sorts of shapes and colours.

As I grew older, so did my ability to see things that other people couldn't but it wasn't until I was about sixteen that it began to dawn on me that I had paranormal powers. It became clear to me that I was receiving thoughts and images from my sixth sense and not from the five senses of hearing, sight, smell, taste or touch. I was getting information both from the living – people and places – and from the departed.

By the age of nineteen, I was already giving readings and conducting séances and healing sessions in halls and people's homes. I served a long apprenticeship in these ways before becoming a full time medium and demonstrating my gift of mediumship in theatres and teaching psychic skills at spiritual centres all over the UK and Europe. (My first book *Spirited* charts my psychic awakening and growth from birth to the present and is an autobiographical account of my experiences as a modern day medium.)

Then in 2004 I was asked if I'd like to 'be on television' and to be honest it was something I had never considered before. I thought about it for a while hoping to receive some divine guidance and when none came, I was forced to make a decision. I know I made the right one as my first television series, *Street Psychic*, was well received and helped change many people's perceptions of how a psychic works and the benefits of seeing one. In this programme my task was to walk the streets of different towns and cities in the UK, stopping passers-by and giving them instant readings. It was a tough job and some people told me to 'get stuffed' when I approached them but many more were open enough for me to connect with them. Then after *Street Psychic* I made several other TV programmes including *Psychic School, The Three*

Mediums, with Derek Acorah and Colin Fry, and last but by no means least, *Psychic Detective*.

In *Psychic Detective* I attempt to shed light on cases where traditional investigative methods have failed or where the police have reached a dead end. My aim is to show that there is a huge number of alternative, ethereal ways to solve serious crimes. Spirit guides, visions, vibrations from the victim's clothing or items can be used by psychics like me to divine the vital missing pieces from the jigsaw puzzle be it the identification of the perpetrator or an insight into the nature of the crime or the crime scene itself.

A VERY BRIEF HISTORY OF PSYCHIC INVESTIGATION

The belief that certain people have psychic powers and are able to understand or see things that cannot be understood or experienced with the known senses is centuries old. Just take a look through some history books and you'll see that many early civilisations from tribal cultures to the ancient Greek and Roman societies, not only acknowledged that such powers existed but elevated those who possessed them to positions of great authority and influence. The concept of an 'oracle' is also present in the Bible which contains many accounts of visions received from spirits. In the middle ages, the self-proclaimed mystic Nostradamus produced a volume of prophecies that is still being examined today, while nowadays interest in the paranormal is reflected in countless books, films, TV dramas and documentaries and the vast number of people who – despite countless sources of information and communication at their disposal – continue to seek out mediums and psychics.

Similarly, the use of paranormal power to help solve crimes is not a recent phenomenon. Thousands of years ago without the benefit of today's sophisticated police methods and forensic science techniques, the quest for justice was much tougher than it is today and paranormal assistance was not discounted. In medieval times criminals were sometimes convicted not on the basis of organised evidence gathering or witness statements but through the testimony of spirits. Perhaps the first officially recorded instance of psychic crime solving was in France in 1692 when the King's procurator enlisted the services of a psychic who used the technique of dowsing to successfully solve the sensational meat cleaver murder of a wine merchant and his wife. In the Victorian era as the new spiritualist movement gathered force, adherents communicated with the dead during séances and evenings of séances and paranormal demonstrations were commonplace. Then with the infamous case of Jack the Ripper we have the first major involvement of psychics in a serial murder enquiry and the emergence of the contemporary psychic detective.

Psychic detection was used during both World Wars to track down missing loved ones and by the later part of the twentieth century hundreds of psychics were working regularly with police all over the world. Some of the most notable included Peter Hurkos (1911-1988) who became famous for his involvement in the Charles Manson murders in 1969 and Gerard Croiset (1909-1980) who become an internationally renowned clairvoyant, highly regarded as a police psychic for his ability to find missing people, animals and objects. Today some law enforcement agencies and lawyers continue to maintain close links with psychics in the 'no stone left unturned' approach to crime solving; although their involvement is often kept top secret.

So you see, the use of psychics and mediums like me in criminal investigations is nothing new; in fact it is thousands and thousands of years old. And with the popularity of television shows like NBC's *The Medium*, USA's *The Dead Zone*, and ITV's *The Afterlife*, psychic investigators are once again gathering renewed interest and attention. And I'm hoping that this attention will lead to greater acceptance, or at the very least greater open mindedness.

Over the years I've grown used to the scepticism, distrust and misgivings that go hand in hand with the work of the psychic detective. In fact I welcome it as the potential for fraud, abuse and foul play for those with no psychic ability but their own agenda is always there and I certainly wouldn't want us to go back to the dark days when anyone could stand up and say they had a vision or saw a spirit and that could be used as evidence against someone. Whenever I put myself forward or get involved in a case there is bound to be criticism and I accept that just as every psychic detective before me has had to do and every psychic detective after me will have to do. I just try to do my job to the best of my ability and I hope my work and my integrity and the testimony of my clients will speak for me.

In the selected case files that follow, you'll see that I don't necessarily try to solve a case but to give it better focus. I aim to provide new information that can be used to get a case moving in the right direction or to offer much needed comfort and resolution to grieving relatives or loved ones. That's my goal, because I believe it is a realistic goal. My chief concern, however, is to offer support and healing to distressed relatives in the best way I know how by offering them proof that our spirit and human personality do survive after death.

UNCOVERING THE TRUTH

The role of a psychic detective is still cloaked in misinformation and misunderstanding, so my aim throughout this book is to shed light on the confusion, attitudes and issues surrounding my work and the spiritual insights I can bring to a case. How do I regard my work? What methods do I use? How is information relayed to me? Is the information I provide correct? What happens when I think I get it wrong? And, to keep things real, just how valid are the criticisms of sceptics who scoff at the very notion of paranormal powers?

The prospect of facing scepticism or ridicule I must confess places a great burden on me. When a person's life is at stake, or relatives are desperate for answers or clues, the struggle to find practical leads and compelling evidence can create an almost unbearable pressure to perform. (Not to mention the risk I take of placing myself in the firing line if a finger is pointed at a criminal!) Nonetheless, despite the risks and potential downside I believe my destiny is to bring people close to moments of truth, even if that truth is at times controversial or painful. Some of what you read in this book is a snapshot of me just doing my job, working with ordinary people and offering them comfort and answers and some of what you read may appear startling or extraordinary, particularly when open wounds such as the London Bombings are re-examined or notorious case files like Jack the Ripper, but whatever you think or feel as you read I hope that you will allow yourself to remain as open minded as possible and aware that the experiences are mine and those of the people I meet and read for.

I've highlighted some of the downsides but there's no denying my work has its upsides as well. As well as offering new insights or perspectives to a case, psychic detectives can often bring healing to those who are suffering. You'll find us portrayed in countless books and movies and the press just love us. I really hope this book will show you the reality behind all this hype and help you uncover the truth for yourself. At the end of the day I'm just an ordinary person blessed with an extraordinary gift. And if my gift can provide leads, insights, answers or, best of all, the comforting thought that there is an afterlife and that silent witnesses are always present in our lives, watching over and guiding us (and ultimately ensuring justice is done) I could hope for nothing better.

PART ONE:

THE CASE FILES

REECE COLLINS AND KEVIN HICKS

One of the most heart wrenching experiences a family can ever face is when another family member is murdered. Not only is there an empty void that cannot be filled, but also a relentless and never ending onslaught of unanswered questions haunt them. 'Did their loved one suffer?' 'How exactly did they die?' 'Could I have done anything to prevent it happening?' 'Did they know how much I loved them?' 'Will the killer ever be found?'

In any given month hundreds of people go through the devastating experience of a family member meeting an untimely and violent end. Although I am only one person and am limited by the number of people I can see, it gives me enormous satisfaction when I can answer questions and offer comfort through their loved ones in spirit.

In the following psychic investigation, I was able to provide much needed insight into the mysterious death of fifteen-year-old Reece Collins. The insight was valuable for the family because it provided answers and encouraged healing, and their lives have not been the same since. What also makes the case stand out, however, is that it led to another investigation. Around the time Reece disappeared another boy also went missing and the more I worked on Reece's case the more I could see a connection between the two disappearances.

REECE COLLINS (1985, CROYDON)

Reece Collins was just fifteen when his body was discovered by his father in a field a short walk from his home. He was hanging by his neck from a tree. Unable to believe that their confident, happy son had taken his own life Reece's family fought for three long years to overturn the verdict of suicide. They eventually succeeded when the police uncovered new evidence and the High Court reopened the case. An open verdict was recorded.

In 2005 I was asked to read for Reece's father, Roy and Reece's sister, Pipsy. My original intention was to find out all I could to help the family confront their demons but in the process I uncovered something more sinister than I could ever have anticipated.

My first meeting with Roy and Pipsy Collins
When I first met Roy and Pipsy, I had no details whatsoever of the case or about them. I prefer to work this way as too much information on a first meeting

can block my ability to see, hear, feel and sense the spirit person. Roy and Pipsy were quite welcoming but also apprehensive and nervous. I immediately sat down with them and told them not to be afraid and if for any reason they felt uncomfortable during the session we would stop.

No sooner had I started to concentrate on the family, my head began to spin and my throat felt dry and sore. I heard crying and shouting. I knew intense sorrow and anger. There was no doubt in my mind that something terrible had happened to these two people.

'Roy and Pipsy, I am getting a sense of family tragedy; something terrifying, that happened around twenty years ago.'

Roy stared at me with moist eyes. His mouth dropped open and he was speechless.

'I want to talk about a bedroom that has been left virtually untouched.'

Roy and Pipsy continued to stare at me.

'It's hardly been touched; left as it was. Does this mean anything to you?'

'Our son's bedroom was left as it was for many years,' replied Roy cautiously. 'It's used now but for years and years it wasn't.'

'I'm feeling a restriction around my neck; someone struggling to breathe. I don't want to dwell on this too long or be too graphic, but something was tied around his neck. Are you okay?'

Roy and Pipsy both nodded.

'I'm sensing that your son was choked and then suspended. It was two different things. The choking came first and then he was suspended or hung to make it look like suicide.'

'Yes, that's incredible!'

'Would he have been fifteen?'

'Yes, he was coming up to his sixteenth birthday; two months away in fact.'

'Are you his sister?' I asked Pipsy.

Pipsy nodded.

'Am I correct in saying that your mother is alive?'

Again Pipsy nodded.

'He wants to send his love to his mum and to tell her and you that he is okay. He's well.'

Pipsy shook her head in disbelief.

'Roy, are you his father? I wasn't sure at first if you were his uncle or his father but he is telling me that he is your son. I'm getting the feeling that he was a carefree, popular lad who was loved and liked by everyone. You would not expect anything bad to happen to him. Wait he wants to tell you something.'

I closed my eyes and prayed I would be able to feel what happened all those years ago and I heard a voice, the voice of a young boy saying over and over again; 'Never let it be said I had taken my own life.'

Roy buried his face in his hands.

'He's waited a long time to say that. He does not want to be blamed. He does not want you to blame yourselves. He was found in an unusual place wasn't he? A place he shouldn't really have been at that time. I'm seeing open space. I'm seeing woodland.'

An astonished looking Roy told me that twenty years ago he found his fifteen-year-old son, Reece, hanging from a tree in some local woodland.

Roy handed me Reece's door keys; keys he would have had in his pocket at the time of his death. I often work with personal items in my investigations. By holding the object I can sometimes sense what the person was like, what they did and even how they died. Perhaps most important, I can sense how the person felt – the emotions of the person at a particular time. I believe emotions are most strongly 'recorded' in the object.

As I held Reece's keys I could feel myself getting closer and closer to Reece's spirit. I could see him walking without a care in the world.

'He was walking down a street,' I told Roy and Pipsy. 'He recognised someone and this person asked him if he could help look for a dog in the woods. Reece loved animals, especially dogs. He wants to help and goes with him.'

Roy and Pipsy looked anguished but they encouraged me to continue.

'I'm seeing a cluster of five trees. Now the ground leaves me. There is a dip in the ground like a hill. Does this sound familiar?'

Roy looked a little puzzled and told me he wasn't sure.

The image of Reece faded in my mind but something

else took its place; the image of another boy trying to tell me something but I couldn't quite understand.

'Just before we finish, Roy, I need to ask you if any other boys disappeared about the same time as Reece, say within a ten or fifteen mile radius.'

'I think there was a boy who went missing. He's never been found though. His parents are dead now but I'm sure his family still want answers.'

'I'm afraid I need to stop now as I'm not picking up any more and feel tired but I do hope this session has been helpful.'

'It's been unbelievable,' Roy said. 'What you have picked up. I'm sceptical and I've never seen a ghost, as for me "seeing is always believing" you know, but some of the things you said there's no way on God's earth you could have known. You've talked about things I had even forgotten and if I've forgotten how could you know?'

I explained to Roy and Pipsy that the spirits always want to bring clarity and I hope that our first meeting has been helpful. Roy mouthed a silent, but heartfelt, 'yes.'

The next day Roy contacted me and told me he had played the tape of our meeting back to his wife, Rita, and that after hearing it she had broken down and cried with relief. He told me that she had kept her feelings hidden for many years and that was why she hadn't attended the meeting. As I listened to Roy I realised that Reece really needed to bring a feeling of comfort and healing to his heartbroken family. The people who loved Reece knew they couldn't get him back but there was a void in their hearts and it was my job to help them.

Reece's old bedroom
Later in the week I visited Reece's old bedroom hoping to pick up Reece's lingering essence or feel his energy. As I entered the room I sensed that twenty years ago his bed was in a different place – facing the window – and that instead of wallpaper the room was painted blue. Roy told me I was correct on both counts.

I placed some clothes Reece would have worn on my lap and closed my eyes. Images of light and colour and fun flashed before my eyes and for a moment I felt like a happy-go-lucky schoolboy. I knew that Reece was not academic and his teachers always wanted him to concentrate more but for him school, like life, was all about having fun. He couldn't wait to leave school and earn money of his own.

I told Roy what I sensed about Reece and he smiled wistfully in agreement. 'I remember everything about my son. Boy, he could be cheeky at times and I know he played up at school. We all went to Spain the year he died. I can remember him asking me if he could have a beer. I said, okay you're fifteen now and he gave me the biggest grin. Naturally we both got drunk. My wife went ape when she found out.'

I smiled at Roy sensing the enduring bond between

father and son. Close to tears Roy told me that on the evening Reece disappeared he immediately suspected something was wrong because Reece was never late home. He went to the police who said they couldn't help until Reece had been missing for twenty-four hours. After a sleepless night and several more visits to the police station he felt so frustrated he decided to do a search himself. He took his dog for a scout of the local wasteland and as he was walking in the field his dog suddenly shot off into some bushes. Roy told me how he followed his dog and was confronted by the most terrible sight; his son hanging from a tree. Panic-stricken he ran to get help and called the police and then a friend of his wife asking them to come over. When he told his wife both of them lost it; it was like a knife through their hearts.

As Roy described his pain I closed my eyes and saw an image of Reece walking down the street. I could hear the name Reece being called and saw in my mind's eye Reece going over. He was apprehensive but trusting as he knew the person who called him. The vision flickered and then faded and I felt a tightness and bitter dryness in my throat. Everything went black as it all went wrong.

Reeling from the shock of my vision I took a deep breath. If I was going to fit any more pieces of the jigsaw puzzle together I knew that I needed to visit the site of Reece's murder.

*　　*　　*

Five trees

Understandably Roy and Pipsy were nervous about visiting the spot where their beloved Reece died but they agreed to accompany me. As we walked to the wasteland Pipsy told me a lot had changed over the years. New houses had been built and trees had been cut down.

Eventually, Roy found the nearest point to where he discovered his son's body and we all stood there in anxious silence. After a while a sickly blackness came over me and my eyes felt heavy and sore. The atmosphere felt strained. I sensed someone walking with intent. I knew that Reece's murder was not random but calculated. It was well thought out and planned. This person went out with the intention to kill.

'I'm sensing an older man. He was teased a lot by kids. He was known in the area but not liked. Something traumatic happened to turn this man's personality; I think the death of his mother or his father. He felt all alone. Life broke apart for this man. He wore a long coat as I can feel it swishing around my calves; it was a raincoat perhaps a trench coat. This man killed your son. He would have been known to you and your family but not as best mates or family so no need to watch your back. He was more an acquaintance or familiar figure; someone you bumped into now and again.'

Roy was clearly bursting to tell me something so I listened to what he had to say.

'We knew our Reece couldn't have committed suicide because of the belt that he was hanging from. It wasn't his belt or one of ours and was not dirty or damp so must have come from someone else. The police also told us when the case files were reopened that Reece couldn't have climbed the tree to hang himself because the tree was covered in algae and no algae was found on Reece's hands, legs, arms or face.'

The blackness and heaviness pushed down on me again. I told Roy that although I felt this man was a predator who went out that night with the intent to kill there was no sexual motive. I could not sense any sexual violation.

Pipsy sighed with relief and then pointed to a cluster of trees nearby.

'Are those the five trees you spoke about in our first meeting? I've always thought it was there that Reece was killed. We used to play a lot there when we were kids.'

As we approached the cluster of five trees I was convinced this was the place I had seen in my first reading for Roy and Pipsy. I was also convinced from the imprint of the place that this was where Reece had been killed. An imprint is an intensely concen-trated pocket of energy, a site at which some extremely dramatic event or series of events has taken place with such profound impact that the images and emotions from these events literally become a part of the land and the atmosphere at the site itself.

'We've been at cross purposes,' Roy commented. 'I

was thinking of this place and you were thinking of over here.'

'Not really at cross purposes,' I replied. 'In clairvoyance you see what you need to see. I saw this gulley and cluster of trees and then I saw a boy hanging from a tree. I just missed the in-between but things are becoming much clearer now. When Reece arrived here another man joins in the struggle. Reece is being held by his wrists. Reece is strong and brave and puts up a fight but he can't fend off two attackers. He was killed right here and then moved, pulled or carried over there to the tree where he was hung. I feel strongly he passed over before he reached the tree.'

'That's uncanny,' replied Pipsy, her eyes widening. 'I was convinced Reece died here too.'

'Our feelings are the same. Although feelings can't offer solid proof you have to admit it's remarkable we both feel the same. I'm not sure why he was moved but perhaps it was because the attackers heard a noise or because twenty years ago the trees were bigger there and it would be easier to fake a suicide attempt.'

I concentrated hard and tried again to tune into Reece's energy. The chilling and gruesome image of five murdered boys flashed into my mind with Reece as the first. As we left the clearing I was convinced that Reece was the first victim of a multiple killer; someone who killed young men without motive, someone who killed for the sake of killing.

* * *

Master at killing

In my work I often find it very helpful to work with other psychics and mediums. I do this for two reasons; to clarify my instincts and to gain greater insight into a case. It's a case of two minds are better than one. Cassandra Maclaine is a Canadian psychic I've worked with a few times over the years. She often uses the ancient art of numerology to help her tune into her clients when giving readings. In numerology dates and names are reduced to single digit numbers between one and nine, with the exception of eleven and twenty-two. Each number has psychological and spiritual attributes and meanings.

Immediately after my visit to the murder scene I set up a web cam chat with Cassandra. She told me Reece's birth date was an eight, which suggests a strong and positive energy. She also told me the date of Reece's death was a nine and nine is the number of endings. As she tuned into Reece's energy Cassandra then confirmed my suspicion that an older man was involved in the attack and that he may have killed others. There was probably an element of ritual involved in the attack as if something needed to be proved. She then went on to say that the attacker was trying to perfect the art of killing. He wanted to be a master at killing.

Incredible, isn't it. Cassandra and I were thousands of miles apart at the time but we both felt the same sadistic, merciless energy. Cassandra also told me something I hadn't figured out yet. She told me she believed Reece's murderer was dead.

Another victim?
With my conviction strengthened that we were not dealing with an isolated attack I headed towards Croydon Central library. I wanted to see if I could learn anything from newspaper articles published a year or so before and after Reece's death. I was certainly not prepared at this stage to back down from my theory that Reece was the victim of a multiple killer. I also felt honour bound to help Roy and his family. My only concern was what I might find. I didn't want to open old wounds for families already haunted by loss and grief.

The library kindly gave me access to the articles and I settled down to read them using a technique called mind scanning where I allow myself to be guided to important information by spirit energy. As I scrolled through the microfilm I stopped whenever I felt something significant might be uncovered. After a few misses I eventually found a feature describing a boy, about the same age as Reece, who went missing within a few months of Reece's murder. I looked at the photograph of the boy and knew at once that he had passed. I could tell from his eyes and face that he was not coming back. I could also tell that although his body had not been found and he was still a 'missing person', he had died within a few hours of his disappearance.

With the image of this boy firmly in my mind I decided to visit the area he had lived in. I found it pretty quickly and started to walk the route he would have walked many times to his home; this route was surprisingly close to Reece's family home. Suddenly, about one hundred yards from where he lived, I feel a shift in energy. My head started to spin just as it had done when I had had a vision of Reece. I saw this boy approached by two men. The vision faded quickly but I was left with the lingering conviction that there was most definitely a connection between this boy and Reece. I wasn't one hundred per cent sure yet what that connection was so before sharing my conclusions with Roy and his family I decided to ask two of my psychic friends, Carol Bohmer and Mandy Gray, to help bring me clarity.

The three of us met at my house that evening to see if our three minds could work as one. With only newspaper articles about Reece's disappearance to guide them both Carol and Mandy cast their thoughts back twenty years. They sensed the same panic, struggle and violence I had sensed. They also felt that Reece was killed by a man who was an outsider or local joke; the kind of guy who hangs around young boys trying and failing to be their mate. Carol suggested that Reece knew who the man was. Mandy sensed that Reece may have agreed to go with him to the woods because he was promised some cash if he did something; perhaps look for a dog or run an errand.

After the meeting with Carol and Mandy I was more convinced than ever that I had useful and important information to offer Roy and his family. A meeting was arranged with Roy and Pipsy and Rita (Reece's mother), who had surprised me by agreeing to attend.

Meeting and healing with the Collinses

I was nervous meeting up with the Collinses for the final time as I had no idea how they would take the news I was about to break to them. The family had been nothing but gentle, open and helpful during what must have been an incredibly painful investigation and I desperately wanted to offer them comfort. I was pleased that Rita had come along, as I knew from my contact with Reece's spirit how close his bond had been with her.

Roy, Pipsy, Rita and myself all sat round the table. I noticed how grief had deeply affected Rita, as though it had been etched across her face.

'This is perhaps one of the hardest cases I have ever worked on because a child is involved, your child, but you need to know that Reece was in the wrong place at the wrong time. If he hadn't been murdered that day another boy would have. Reece was courageous and strong and he put up a fight but I want you to know that his passing was quick; so quick, in fact that when he passed over to the spirit world he had to be told what happened to his body by his friends and family in the other world. He didn't even know that he was found hanging from a tree. It's really important that I tell you this. His passing was quick and he is with friends and family now.'

Roy and Rita looked visibly relieved. As I talked I felt Reece's spirit coming closer and closer.

'I don't believe in heaven or hell but in a spirit world. I want to tell you that Reece's killer is dead but before he passed he killed three or four more times. There is another boy who went missing around the same time in your area and I feel a strong connection between his disappearance and Reece's murder. In the spirit world Reece's killer is going to have to come to terms with what he has done and it won't be easy for him I can guarantee you that. He is in a very, very dark place.' At this point I took a deep breath as I felt some of the killer's heaviness and blackness bearing down on me.

'I want you to know that Reece is being looked after in spirit. He's surrounded by people who love him and he wants you to know he is okay. He also wants you to know that he is linked to you eternally and that bond will never be broken. Please be aware of his presence in your dreams or in the real world when things go click or thud or when you feel a breath of air on your cheek. He has been finding it hard to get through to you and he just wants you to say "hello, how are you" sometimes.'

With that I closed the meeting and thanked Reece's spirit and my guides. I also added a special prayer in my heart for the Collins family to use the information

I had given for their healing. I knew my prayer was answered because, as they were leaving, Rita turned to me with tears in her eyes and said, 'Now I can go to bed not thinking about him hanging in that tree. I feel much lighter. Thank you.'

'Thank you,' echoed Roy. 'Knowing Rita feels better helps me. I've seen her suffer for so long.'

'The hatred is still there,' Rita added, 'but it's going down. It's never going to go completely away but knowing the killer is dead makes it easier.'

Roy looked at his wife and daughter and then to me. 'Your words were good words, helpful words. It will change things for us knowing our boy didn't suffer for long. It makes it easier knowing he is okay now and still around us.'

There was no doubt that the investigation into the death of Reece Collins had been traumatic and intense for us all but as I waved goodbye to the family I knew healing had begun. The great joy for me here was not only to be able to enlighten a family drowning in grief about the truth of life after death but also to have the privilege of witnessing the beginning of miraculous change in them all because of it.

KEVIN HICKS

I was thrilled to witness the beginning of healing for the Collins family but over the next few weeks I couldn't shake the case from my mind; in particular its connection with the other missing boy. A few months later a quiet but confident woman approached me after a public demonstration of mediumship in Croydon, asking for help. Her name was Alex Hicks and she was the sister of Kevin Hicks; the boy who had gone missing around the same time as Reece.

Meeting Alex was a reassuring and wonderful example of synchronicity; something that happens a lot in my life. The spirits had guided both of us together and there was no question in my mind that Alex and her family needed my help. I agreed to do a reading for her. As I began to tune into her energy I noticed an old man standing on her right side. I began to describe this man to Alex, a man I knew nothing of prior to this sitting.

'I have a gentleman here who gives you a lot of love. He's a well-built man with beautiful blue eyes, and he's smoking a cigarette. I feel his tummy may have poured a little over his belt. I think he's your maternal grandfather. Does that make sense to you?'

Alex nodded and for the first time since our meeting gave me a shy smile.

'There are lots of memories he talks to me of here, him being a big man in his chair and you as a child being near him and sitting on his knee and him giving you a kiss. He likes to kiss and cuddle this man and tickle and play games with you. Games like balancing a spoon on his nose.'

'Yeah, that's right.'

'I think your mother wants to come forward now. Your grandfather is helping her come forward. She is saying sorry to you a lot. I think she passed with a heart condition or a breathing problem. She keeps saying sorry because she felt that she pushed you away and wouldn't allow you to get close to her. She's opposite to the way your grandfather was. He was very demonstrative.'

Alex looked down to the floor in sadness.

'She is very different but I feel she got like this after your brother went missing. She was never the most demonstrative person but the shock of his disappearance made her worse. But don't think he was her favourite she says. You are not to think that.'

Alex's eyes started to go moist. 'Yes, I understand.'

'In life you had a closer bond with your dad. He was called John wasn't he?'

'That was his name.'

'He was a funny man with a great sense of humour. He loved your mum but the two of them were so different. Your mum was forever tidying and cleaning, washing and scrubbing but before she passed she gave up and just sat in a chair. She tells me she gave up on life and she could have stayed longer but decided not to. I am not saying that she took her own life but she willed death upon herself. Is that making sense to you?'

'It most certainly does,' replied Alex quietly.

'Your mother passed before your father but they

are very close to each other in the spirit world now. She's talking about the porch door?'

'It was always left open.'

'I feel it was left open not just for any reason but in case your brother came home. That's why it was always left open. I feel that your mother was left with lots of "if onlys" because when he disappeared she had asked your brother to run an errand for her and go to the shops.'

Alex's eyes brightened. 'That's the truth.'

'Your brother was near a parade of shops just before he vanished. There's something about baking a cake. She had been shopping that day but had forgotten eggs or butter or something. Now going to your brother; he's here now and I feel him to have been around sixteen when he passes.'

'He was sixteen when we saw him last.'

'I think he was quite a sensible boy in his lifetime. I do feel he is in the spirit world. I feel he would have gone missing somewhere near the shops because shops are very important to him. Do you think I might be wrong?'

'No, you are very right.'

'Whilst at these shops I suddenly need to go to the back of the shops. Do you know if he had any friends that lived at the back of the shops or maybe a couple of streets back?'

'Yes, there's one who lived half way down from the shops.'

I felt a slight pressure on my chest as the image of Kevin came back to me stronger and clearer than ever before. 'He's showing me something from earlier in the day. He went missing after dinner at around six thirty p.m. but he is showing me about four o'clock and I feel that he is seeing the people that later on would have been involved in his disappearance. There is a car, there is a younger guy driving with an older guy in the passenger seat and he thinks they are up to something because they drive very slowly. I don't wish to make a connection here with Reece and your brother if it is not true, but I saw them speaking to Reece about a dog, saying we are looking for our dog and they are doing the same to Kevin. The car that I am seeing is an estate four-door car, grey black or grey blue in colour. As your brother sees these people he thinks they are odd, but he doesn't think any more about it and he goes about his business. That's important. There is something about first contact with these people and I feel the second time your brother went out they were still in the area. And I feel that he was able to speak to them easier because he felt he had a connection. Do you understand?'

Alex's face went white as she nodded.

'Your brother is telling me that there are two people who abducted him. He is telling me something about a park. There is water. The water is very shallow. Do you remember if he was wearing a white shirt when he vanished?'

'He was wearing a white T-shirt and the jacket was partly white.'

'I feel they take Kevin in their car to a wood and he is killed near the trees but his body is moved somewhere else. There are two perpetrators and another who looks like an onlooker, only he is a young kid. I'm getting the name Christopher. I'm seeing water. There is a very big tree here to my right-hand side. The details aren't clear but I can tell you your brother is in the spirit world. It might be best now if you asked me some questions.'

Alex began to move uneasily in her chair. What I had been saying to her had clearly hit a nerve.

'You said he was killed in one place and then was taken to another. Christopher was a friend of Kevin's and we think he may have been involved. We've been trying to find him for years but he has vanished, even the police cannot find him. Do you know where he is?'

'When I ask in my head all I get is Brighton.'

'We've tried there but have had no luck. Do you know if any of the people involved are still living?'

I knew what I was about to tell Alex wouldn't be easy to hear so I concentrated hard to make sure I was absolutely certain before I replied. 'I believe that one of them is still living and what's more I believe that the same people that killed Reece also killed your brother.'

With that the session ended. I was concerned that

all this was a lot to take on board but Alex assured me even though there were many unanswered questions she had found the session helpful and she was keen to meet up again. She recognised the personalities coming through in many things that were said and was comforted by the thought that Kevin was being well cared for in the spirit world.

THE TAKING OF LIFE

I want to conclude this chapter with some thoughts about the spirit world and murder. Taking the life of another before his or her time is a devastating and horrific act that appears totally unforgivable and when murder is the case there is the additional sense that justice must be served. As I believe one of those involved in the deaths of Reece and Kevin is still alive few of you reading this would not wish for some kind of retribution for that individual. This is understandable but I ask you to pause for a moment and glance at the situation from a spiritual rather than an emotional point of view.

Please understand that I'm not condoning murder in any way; I want to make it clear that someone who takes the life of another commits a reprehensible and unacceptable wrong that causes pain and confusion both in this world and the next. Death or punishment, however, isn't vindication in the spirit world as so many believe it can be in life. In the spirit world the mindset of anger and hatred that controls a murderer takes them to a realm where others of a similar mindset dwell and they will remain there until their spirits can evolve to an awareness of their wrongdoing and a realisation that life is not theirs for the taking. Until they can take that step, whether they are living in this world or the next, the souls of people who intentionally and callously take the life of another remain unevolved and tormented – and there can be no greater punishment or suffering than that.

2

THE LONDON BOMBINGS

Although the spirit world didn't give me any direct warnings about the London Bombings, for much of my life, growing up in the East End, I lived with a sense of anxiety and foreboding about underground trains and black travel bags that only really made sense to me in the weeks following 7/7.

I have an especially powerful and vivid memory that dates back to 1979, when I was about ten. I was travelling on the underground with my Auntie Grace to Leyton. It was during the time of the IRA threat to London so bombs were very much a talking point. At one point in the journey my heart beat so loud I wondered why everyone in the carriage couldn't hear or feel it too. It felt stiflingly hot and my Auntie thought I might be coming down with something. I clearly remember her holding her hand to my damp forehead and sighing with concern. Cuddling up to my Auntie for comfort I glanced at the bags and cases people had carried onto the train and for an instant these practical travelling accessories seemed to take up the whole carriage making it impossible for me to move or even breathe. Thankfully Leyton was the next stop and my legs felt so weak that I had to be helped out of my seat to leave the train. For months after I had recurring nightmares about tube trains, intense heat and trying to catch my breath. Sometimes I'd wake up in a cold sweat and it would take several hours for the fear to leave me. And for years afterwards black bags or backpacks never failed to trigger irrational feelings of anxiety whenever I spotted them in the street or on a train, bus, plane or tube.

About ten days before 7/7, I had an extremely intense nightmare. In my dream I saw myself walking along a tube station and stepping inside a train. As the doors shut I sat down and there was a large black bag between my legs. I immediately panicked as it didn't belong to me and then I woke up struggling to breathe and sweating with my heart beating fast and loud. At the time I didn't pay much attention to the dream as I had had similar dreams since childhood but what made this dream stand out is that it was so persistent. For the next two nights I had exactly the same dream; something that had never happened before.

On the morning of 7/7 I remember waking up very early feeling tired and unsettled. I found it hard to think about the day ahead and had no appetite for my breakfast, which is unusual for me as I'm very much a morning person. Then I switched on the radio to hear the announcer say that three underground trains at King's Cross, Edgware Road and Aldgate East had been involved in explosions of some sort and that a Number 30 bus that was going from Marble Arch to Hackney had had its roof blown off in Tavistock Square.

Suddenly everything clicked; my childhood memories, recurring nightmares and the unsettled feeling since I woke up. Everything made sense in that instant. I believe that all thoughts create energy in the cosmos and over the years – and more intensely in recent weeks – some part of me must have been tuning into the thoughts and actions of the terrorists as plans were thought up and executed for this horrific act. What was extraordinary too was that in the days after the bombing the familiar feeling of foreboding that had haunted me for twenty or so years whenever I was in or near tubes or saw black bags was replaced by feelings of incredible sadness and love. The sadness was natural and to be expected but I didn't expect to feel such overwhelming love. It wasn't until a few weeks later that I fully appreciated the significance of this feeling.

Back to the morning of 7/7; like many Londoners on that day I was glued to the television set but I also had to go about my business as usual. It was impossible, however, not to think about the suffering and confusion that friends and family of missing loved ones must have been going through as formal identification of the victims was going to take a very long time. I desperately wanted to help and the spirits answered my prayers. I had to drop off some photos to be developed that morning and as I went into the shop I could sense that the woman at the desk was agitated. I asked her if she was okay and she looked at me with fear in her eyes. She explained that she had not heard from her son and didn't know if he was dead or alive as he travelled on the tube into King's Cross every morning.

Although I rarely give impromptu readings, on that unique day I was so touched by her devastation that something made me reach out and hold her hand. I wasn't asking the spirits for anything but as I held her hand I felt a cold shiver down my spine. Without thinking I told her that her son would be fine and that she would know he was okay by 12.40 that afternoon. Gulping back tears the woman smiled at me and I could feel some of the tension leave her.

The next day I went back to collect my photos and the same woman was at the desk. She was delighted to see me and told me that her son had called her at exactly 12.40 yesterday to tell her he was okay. He hadn't been able to call her immediately because he had been dangerously close to the tragedy. Clearly still in a state of shock the woman asked me how I knew he would be okay and the time he would call. I told her that with an open mind and a strong desire to know the truth wonderful things can and do happen.

When tragedy or disasters strike one of the questions I'm often asked is: If you're a psychic why didn't you see this coming. The answer is that I am not aware of all things and nor should I be, if I was constantly open to every good or bad thing that was to happen, I simply wouldn't be able to comprehend it all and would certainly shut off psychically all together. Much as I'd like to be able to predict future tragedies and prevent pain and suffering my own higher self wouldn't allow me to do this as it would be wrong; possibly even harmful to our spiritual growth. All of life is about learning from experiences and some of those experiences will be positive and some will be negative.

Do some things happen for a reason, even things that seem unjust and terrible? Perhaps we should try to understand the duality of nature as it is through the negative that the positive can be appreciated. I believe our lives are part of a much bigger picture and it is only in spirit that we can begin to understand this. Bearing all this in mind, was 7/7 in some way a wake up call to the world about injustice and pain that has been hidden for too long? Will the event be valuable in our spiritual growth? Will it be a catalyst for change or greater tolerance? Will it bring people closer together? Such questions can't be answered with our rational minds; they can only be answered spiritually.

Accepting that things happen for a reason may seem impossible for someone who is grieving the loss of a loved one but as you will see from the following reading that is what the spirits would like us to do. When the reading was over, I noticed a complete change in the parents. They were still crying but there was a glimmer of hope in their eyes.

MY READING WITH JUNE AND JOHN TAYLOR

Towards the end of a large demonstration to about 2,000 people in Brentwood, Essex I became aware of a lovely young spirit lady wanting to make contact with her mother. I told the audience that I was receiving information that a mother in the auditorium had lost a daughter. A lot of people stood up but many sat down when I said the young lady's name felt like Karen or something similar and the initials J and J came to mind. Eventually, only one lady called June Taylor was left standing. I told her that the young lady was about twenty-four and that she had died in tragic circumstances. After the show there were dozens of people waiting to speak to me and one of them was June and her husband, John. As soon as June shook my hand her daughter drew very close to me. I felt compelled to give June my private number so we could organise a meeting at a later date.

At the reading I sat June, John and their son Simon down and explained how I worked. I told them that when I do a reading I try to speak everything that comes through my mind; even if what comes through is painful. I believe that the spirits will only provide me with information that is appropriate for them to hear. I do this because I am a medium and it is not my place to censor information. Therefore I describe my feelings, both good and bad and any visual details, however small, as they may be extremely significant.

I uttered my opening prayer and when it was completed I looked to June's right and saw as I had done in Brentwood the same pretty young girl, aged no more than twenty-three or twenty-four with thick straight hair that was a colourful mixture of blonde and brown. She was holding one hand over her chin as if to hide a blemish on her skin and she was holding a book open in the other.

'I believe your daughter is standing beside you. She is talking about books and exchanging books with you.'

'Yes,' replied June. 'We liked to do that. She was always reading and suggesting books for me to read. She had an open mind and was determined to open mine.'

'I am feeling that she worked very hard at her studies but never felt she was going to do well, but she always did. I'm getting the name Carrie now. Is her name Carrie or Karen?'

John smiled in agreement. 'She was called Carrie but when we went on holiday in America her name was often misspelled as Karen.'

'She's telling me she loved her new job. She also

says that she liked to party but sometimes she liked to be alone too. She loved chilling out in her bedroom and Saturday afternoon was her favourite time to relax. I'm getting some kind of problem with her chin, it feels sore. She was also worried about her weight wasn't she, June?'

'That's incredible,' said June. 'She had only just started a new job and yes she did have a little irritation on her chin. Although she was tall and slim, she thought she needed to lose weight, but she didn't. Girlie stuff really; the two of us would compare tummies, but I always knew I would win.'

As June spoke with such tenderness and a hint of humour the image of Carrie grew sharper in my mind. I could see her holding an animal that looked like a rabbit. I told June and John about the rabbit and how chuffed Carrie felt to be holding it again.

'Oh my God!' cried June. 'When our rabbit died she was so upset.'

'It's not just a rabbit who's with her,' I said. 'She's got your father there too, John, and he is taking care of her. She looks more like John than you June, am I correct?'

'Yes,' replied June. 'She was the image of her dad. She was close to us all in different ways but it was her dad that she would go to the pictures with and her dad she would stay up late at night chatting to.'

'But she is really close to you as well June.' I replied. 'She knows you wake up every morning at four a.m.

thinking about her. She knows you light a candle and bring her fresh flowers. She knows you haven't got rid of anything that is hers, even her make-up. She knows your sadness.'

June nodded silently and I could see a tear slip down her cheek.

'I'm telling you that a week or so before she died she thought a lot about the meaning of life and life after death. She says she was glad she always told people how much she loved them. She loves her brother. She wants you to know that. I can see her wrapping her arms around him as if to protect him.'

Simon stared at the floor and whispered. 'I miss her terribly, as we all do.'

'She's moving closer to you now John. She is telling me about a key-ring. Do you have something of hers on your key-ring?'

'Yes, I do. I'm driving her car and it's her trinket on the key-ring.'

'She's talking about liver and onions now.'

'Oh God,' replied June, almost giggling. 'John and Carrie loved liver and onions but I hated it. I would never cook the onions because they made me cry.'

'She wants you to wear her ring June. The one she was given for her eighteenth or twenty-first birthday. And she wants John to keep the key-ring too. This is important to her. She is also telling me that you have seven photographs of her in your lounge but there is one in which she looks very formal. She doesn't like that one as much as the others. June, she's telling me now that you rung her up on her mobile. She really wanted to answer but couldn't. I don't want to create problems here, but Carrie is telling me that when she died she was cradled in the arms of a lady but it's strange because her death could have been prevented if help had got to her sooner. I'm getting the number twenty-three. I'm also getting transport, speed, noise, metal and Liverpool Street.'

'Every morning on a weekday I'd walk with Carrie to Liverpool Street,' whispered June. 'Then . . . .' and her voice faltered.

'Carrie died in the London bombings,' interrupted John. 'Nobody was expecting this and they couldn't get help down fast enough. They took twenty-three minutes to reach her but once they did she died after four minutes. They got to her too late.'

John reached out to hug his wife and she put her head in her hands and said quietly. 'In those hours when we didn't know where she was or what had happened I rang her mobile over and over again. The helpline number they gave me was useless, so as we called hospitals and police stations I had her number on redial. The police still haven't given us back her mobile phone.'

I could sense that Carrie wanted to change the mood. It was growing too dark for her and she wanted it lighter. 'She is thinking about Tenerife now,' I said. 'She doesn't want to think about how she died she wants you all to remember Tenerife.'

'We all went on holiday there when she was young,' said June with a whisper of a smile.

'I can feel lots of spirit people coming in to support her. She is showing me her nails and is telling me she has lovely ones now. She wants you to know she is very happy and being looked after in the spirit world. She is very close to your mother June, which is beautiful because she didn't get the chance to be close to her in life. The spirits keep saying history is repeating itself. I feel your mother died when you were twenty-three or twenty-four, just as Carrie passed over at this age?'

'I was twenty-three when my mother died,' whispered June. 'My mum will probably spoil her rotten.'

'June, forgive me for being so direct but the spirits know that you have come close to ending it all but I want to tell you that when you were at your lowest last year your mother and Carrie were with you and they are always with you.'

June lifted her head and whispered, 'Thank you.'

'John you go walking a lot, don't you?'

'Yes, when I want to be alone I like to walk and walk.'

'I know, your daughter is acknowledging what seems to be a lot of walking on your own and I know that she is picking up on that. She says to me when you walk you don't walk alone because she walks with you and even though you think you are on your own she wants you to feel her there with you.'

'I do. I can often feel her presence. She is always in my thoughts. Never a day or hour or second goes by without her being there,' replied John.

'Know that it is not imagination, it is her. She keeps saying to me I will be with him especially when the bluebells are out. Does that mean anything?'

'We have bluebells in our garden,' answered John.

'I know that she doesn't want you to go over and over the tiniest part of her life which is the end bit. She wants to talk about everyday happy things that remind you of her such as liver and onions, reading Harry Potter, biting her nails, worrying about exams, her jewellery, worrying about her weight and drinking hot chocolate and eating raw carrots.'

'She loved to sit on the sofa with a cup of chocolate and when I cooked she would always eat raw carrots. Those are happy memories,' replied June.

'Although she wants you to focus on the everyday things she does also want you to know about her last day too as she believes it will help you move forward. Something hit her head and she was standing not sitting when the bomb exploded. Before she passed away she tried to get a message to you.'

'Yes,' said John, sighing. 'The ambulance worker said she was trying to speak but it didn't make sense as she was slipping in and out of consciousness.'

'Well, I can tell you what she was trying to say. She was sending a message of love and she is sending a message of love to you right now. She wants you to know she is okay and she wants everyone to treat themselves to some chocolate.'

'She was always buying little treats like that for us. That sounds so much like her,' laughed John.

As my link to the spirit world faded I saw Carrie once more holding an open book in her hands and reading. I closed the session and asked John, June and Simon if they had found it helpful.

'Incredibly,' said June. 'You have no idea how much hope you have given us. You take it all for granted when you are alive but then when you lose someone special you can't tell them what you wanted to tell them. When she went like that we couldn't even see her at the hospital and say our goodbyes but I feel better now that I know she is happy and has got everybody with her. I needed that to go on because I can't bear to think about her up there on her own. This is the best present, the greatest comfort I've had since she died. Thank you.'

'I wasn't sure about life after death,' added John, 'but things have happened recently to challenge all that. Carrie's number came up once on Simon's phone and then there was the smell of burning candles. We have never smelt that smell before or since, but just after she died we smelt it around six times. Then when you spoke to us at Brentwood I was amazed and what you have said today has been spot on. It's as if she is here with us right now.'

As we spoke I could understand and feel the pain and anger in their voices but I could also see that their love for her and each other was stronger than their hurt.

'You know the saddest thing,' said June, 'is that most of her friends come from ethnic minorities. She would sometimes have a go at me because she said I was judgemental and shouldn't judge a book by its cover. She always defended the minority and would champion their rights and their differences. She would take each person on merit as a human being. She was such a special, beautiful girl. She didn't deserve to die.'

I told June, John and Simon about the strong image I had at the end of the reading of Carrie with an open book as if she was urging not just her parents but everyone to set aside their differences and open their minds.

'Yes,' interrupted John. 'We have met so many families affected by the bombings and many come from totally different backgrounds and cultures. And we have all become incredibly close. Differences, beliefs and culture don't come into it. We're united by our humanity and by our loss. I think that religion and politics has been at the root of so many evil things over the centuries.'

I could not help but agree. 'Take religion and let's just leave us with humanity and spirituality,' I said. 'I think we would all get on a lot better.'

A few months later June got in touch to tell me that she had started writing, dedicated to Carrie. Here's a brief sample.

Pre 7/7 our world complete not knowing
devastation, we lived life to the full no
fear of Aldgate Station, life now for us
is day by day, our dreams and plans as
dust, we all take life a little slower
as all involved know we must. How do you
replace perfection say all who knew her?
You just remember all the times as this
is the final connection.

We wait, we sit and wonder a sign is what
we need, we're all at sea with no direction;
will someone please take heed, we're lost
and feeling incomplete our world no longer
perfect we need your strength to muddle
through back then it all seemed worth
it. We wonder now what way is ours a
journey never travelled, we stand together
hand in hand until all will be unravelled.

Today we celebrate our life, tomorrow may
be too late, so love and embrace your
kids, your partner, even your best mate.
Don't take for granted what you have but
treasure every minute for when the day
comes to a close you don't know who's left
in it.

As I read her words from the heart I could sense that Carrie was moving June towards new spiritual heights and that not just June but all who read her poems would benefit.

WHY US AND NOT THEM?

One of the reason events like 7/7 terrify us is that any one of us could have been on that tube or bus if we had had business in London on that day. Why did some people step onto the tube or bus targeted by the bombers? Why did Carrie have to die and not the person in the carriage behind? Why did others oversleep or get delayed or change their plans so they missed the train or bus they might normally catch? In short, why did certain people die that day and why did others survive? Since 7/7 I've been asked this question over and over again. There are no easy answers but I really feel the following true story is significant in some way.

Samantha is a good friend of mine who lives and works in King's Cross as both a PR consultant and part-time actress. Every morning she leaves her flat at the same time to grab a coffee and buy a paper before getting on the Number 30 bus to work. On the morning of 7/7 something very unusual happened. Her cat jumped in front of her as she tried to leave. Although he had already been fed he ran in and out of her legs and purred loudly making it impossible for Samantha to open her front door. The purring was so endearing and unusual as her cat is normally very independent and not keen on being fussed over that Samantha went back into her flat and topped up her cat's food bowl and changed his water.

After giving her cat a stroke Samantha finally left her flat again and started to walk her normal route. She was about five minutes behind schedule and realised she needed to hurry to make up time. Just as she began to jog to the bus stop she heard a very loud bang. It was the explosion caused by the bomber sitting on the Number 30 bus; a bus Samantha could well have been on if she had not been delayed. Later that afternoon she called me in tears and told me how close she had been to tragedy.

What makes this story remarkable is that Samantha's cat had not ever acted that way before or since. Animals are often used by spirit to get our attention in some way and in this instance Samantha was sensitive enough to respond. I truly believe that we are all born with a spirit or sixth sense but increasingly as we grow older and the pressures of materialism and modern life bear down on us we lose touch with our innate sensitivity. On that morning Samantha listened to her heart not her watch and it may just have saved her life.

This isn't to say that those who died on 7/7 didn't listen to their feelings; quite the opposite may in fact have been the case. Who knows why some die on a particular day in a particular way and some do not? I believe that in life we are learning from experience and certain advanced souls may have agreed in advance to leave this world in a certain manner to help them in their spiritual growth; perhaps to gain a clearer insight into love and an appreciation of life or perhaps to raise universal consciousness and a desire for unity in others. Only one thing is certain, our lives are part of something much greater than we can fathom in this life and the souls that passed that day passed for reasons that will only become clear in spirit.

The following reading is another wonderful example of how a spirit attempts to comfort loved ones by showing that our souls grow the most under the greatest of stress. All that matters is the amount of love that we have in our hearts; as love is indestructible in both this life and the next.

READING WITH KIM

I got in touch with Kim via *Spirit and Destiny* magazine who asked me to do a series of readings for them. Unknown to me Kim had tried to contact me before for a reading but this hadn't been possible because of my lengthy waiting list. She was very pleased then when *Spirit and Destiny* called out of the blue and asked her to take part in a reading with me. Before I met Kim I had no idea who she was and why she needed my help.

After spending a few moments putting Kim at ease and explaining how I like to work, the image of a man sitting on a couch sprang into my mind.

'I think your father is here, sitting to your right. He is telling me you are the image of him, Kim, is that correct?' I asked.

Kim looked to the right and hesitantly replied, 'I'm not sure. My dad died when I was eighteen months so I never really knew him.'

'Your dad wants you to know he's watched you growing up. He's always been with you. There's another spirit here with him but it's not your mum. It's some-one older, someone who felt like she was your mum but wasn't. Does that make sense?'

'Yes,' replied Kim. 'It was Nan really who brought me and my sister Lin up.'

'Your nan was a very capable woman. She liked a clean house didn't she? Not like your mum who is, how can I put it, a little less tidy.'

Kim nodded.

'I'm getting the number seventy-four. Did your nan pass when she was seventy-four?'

'She was exactly seventy-four. That's remarkable!'

'She was a small woman with a large chest. I hope I'm not being rude here?'

'No, not at all,' grinned Kim.

'I think your nan missed you terribly when you moved out. The last six years of her life were quite lonely; all that noise and company and then quiet.'

'I know she missed us,' said Kim sadly.

'Don't feel sad for her,' I replied. 'She knows that it was right for you to leave. She's not upset with you. She's happy for you and so proud. She's telling me that she is sorry that your mother hasn't been there for you but then your mother has always been a law unto herself. She wants you to look out for your mum right now as she has got some kind of chest infection?'

Kim nodded and as she did the spirit of a young man came through loud and clear. 'Your nan is step-ping aside now and a young man is stepping forward,' I said. 'Someone who was too young to pass; he's trying to sit on your lap Kim. He's far too old to do that but that's what he is trying to do. He is making me laugh. He's got a sense of humour this one; a cheeky side to him. He's about twenty-three and he is calling you his mum. His passing was so sudden there was no time to say goodbye. I am seeing sharp objects, metal, hearing noise and I can see him falling down. His passing was sudden, almost too sudden.'

Kim rubbed her face with her hands as I spoke. 'It's Phil! My youngest son, Phil. He died in the London bombings.'

'He's got some scissors and he is going on about hair or cutting hair. Does this mean anything to you?'

'He was a hairdresser,' answered Kim.

'He is wearing jeans and has two tattoos on his arm. I can see him with a pint, mucking about and singing with his mates. I can see he has a gold earring. He's digging me on the face now. Did he have a mole? There was a dimple on his chin and he had brown hair and brown eyes. He was lovely and had a wicked sense of humour. He loved life but goodness did he swear a lot. He wants to say sorry for the pain you are going through. He knows you were heartbroken when he died. He was your baby. Does this make sense?'

'Yes, everything,' replied Kim. 'Phil was my youngest boy and I never thought I would have him. I've got four other children and he was spoiled rotten being the youngest. The others used to say he could get away with anything but they never got angry with him. You couldn't get angry with Phil he was so full of life, so full of fun. A total nutter at times but everyone loved him.'

'I'm getting the name of a pub, the Baker something. I can see him laughing again with a pint in his hands. He's living a good life in spirit. He's got your dad and your nan with him.'

'The Baker's Arms was his local and yes everything's spot on. My Phil lived life to the full,' Kim interrupted.

'He is also talking about a mate of his who passed before him. The two of them are together now and they are having a great time. I'm getting the name Daniel.'

'Daniel,' said Kim hesitantly and then her eyes lit up. 'Daniel died a few years ago. They were best mates. Daniel died suddenly, very suddenly. I know Phil missed him.'

I looked at Kim and heard Phil again. 'He says he will be with you when you want him. He'll be with you when you need him. He will always be with you. There's a mark on his head but he says it was a bit of a fiddle or a muddle when he passed.'

'Yes, there have been a lot of enquiries. He did have head injuries but they aren't sure if that is what killed him,' replied Kim.

'Phil says he doesn't want you living a life of trying to find vengeance. He says he shouldn't have been there in the first place but don't be leading a bitter life trying to find answers as spirit will sort it out. There's an urn where you keep his ashes isn't there? You haven't scattered them yet have you?'

'That's right. I don't know how you knew that.'

'He says it's fine to scatter them whenever you feel ready. He'll be with you when you do. He wants you to know that he loved his life, loved you and didn't want to pass over but now that he has gone he wants you to stop being sad because he died. He hates it when you are sad.'

As the meeting drew to a close I saw Phil gently stroking his mother's hair. Kim was a remarkably strong woman who had been to hell and back but I could see that Phil's connection with her was giving her strength and the love Kim was sending Phil was giving him spiritual strength. Kim wanted to know if her son felt pain when he died. I told her that spirits often tell me that when death is sudden it can take a while to realise what has happened. It is only when they see their lifeless form that they understand they have died. Fortunately, in such cases when a spirit is jolted out of its body there is always a relative or friend or guide nearby to assist them through the transition and Phil was surrounded by spirit people who loved and cared for him.

I also told Kim that with any death, in particular one like Phil's that was sudden, a spirit would need time and help to adjust but that there were always beautiful souls on hand to help them. If a person dies without warning and there isn't time for goodbyes this can be a terrible thing for both spirit and those left behind. Kim had tried to contact Phil in spirit and Phil had been reaching out to her but I explained to her that contact had not been established until now because it was all too soon. Phil needed a period of adjustment to his new life in spirit and Kim needed to come to terms with his death. Now both were ready to be reunited. In both life and death love was binding them together.

After the meeting Kim told me that her son was such a character that everyone said he should be a celebrity. He always wanted to be a star and in the months after his death she had been overwhelmed by the support and love she had received from people all over the world. There had been hundreds and hundreds of cards and well wishes. In both life and death he was her star.

Kim also told me she had bonded with other grieving relatives of the London Bombings. This is significant because if any good at all comes out of such injustice it is perhaps that in those terrible times people join together in their sense of outrage, shock and grief and that someone else's loss – Kim's loss, June, John and Simon's loss – becomes for a moment our loss, everyone's loss. In other words with the help of loved ones who have passed over we are all united and undivided in the love we have for one another. And in this unity there is the hope that good will always triumph over hate and injustice.

The desire to see someone pay for their crime is a powerful one but I know without a doubt that revenge or retaliation for those who willingly hurt innocents was not the way forward. Healing could only be found in spirit and in love. Love begets love and it survives death. Those we love never leave us and the more people we love in our lives the easier it is to recognise loved ones in the eyes of others, even strangers. Both good things and terrible things happen on earth but one thing never changes and that is the power of love. Love, in both this life and the next, is eternal and because it works to unite us rather than divide us it is the ultimate power and only truly effective weapon against hate.

3

NOAH AND ANGEL

When writing this book I had to look though several years of readings in order to present to you what I felt were unique examples of my psychic investigative work. In my research a number of cases stood out from the rest and the following is one of them because in my opinion it is a remarkable demonstration not just of the power of spirit but of the power of love that survives death.

PLEASE HELP ME!

Several years ago I received a letter from a Nigerian women living in south London. The letter was written on a scrap of paper and I had to read it several times as it was quite difficult to read at first. I assumed that whoever wrote it must have been in an awful hurry. Enclosed in the envelope were two small passport sized photographs of a young girl and boy.

Dear Mr Stockwell

I have heard of your work and am in desperate
need of your help. My children are missing and
no one will help me find them. I don't know
what to do and I'm scared. The police aren't
interested and you are my last hope. If you
think you can help me please call the number
below. Yours . . .

I called the number scribbled on the bottom straight
away.

The phone was picked up almost immediately by
a woman who answered in a language I couldn't
understand but when I said, 'Hello, it's Tony Stockwell
here. I got your letter,' she spoke in English and told
me her name was Pearl. She had a strong Nigerian
accent which was at times very hard for me to understand, especially when she began to cry, but one thing
I did hear loud and clear because she said it so many
times was; 'My babies have been taken, oh my God,
please you must help me. Will you help me?'

Normally, I can't respond to personal requests
immediately as my reading and touring schedule is
planned and booked months and now years in
advance but I was so touched by Pearl's distress that
without hesitation I arranged to meet her at South
Kensington station the very next morning.

After saying goodbye to Pearl and putting the phone
down my eyes were immediately drawn to the two

small photographs of the missing children she had enclosed with her letter. I picked them up and as soon as I did the word 'Noah' and a vision of a white angel came into my mind. Wondering if Pearl was deeply religious and the thoughts and pictures that came to me were connected with her devotion, I put the photos in my coat to make sure I would not forget them the following day.

As I approached South Kensington station the next morning the place was crowded and busy as always but when I saw a lady standing alone with a well used handkerchief in her hand and a look of intense pain etched across her face I knew straight away that this had to be Pearl. There was a nip in the air and spots of rain were starting to fall so I suggested we went to a coffee shop nearby.

Pearl agreed and we sat down and ordered some hot drinks. I asked her to tell me the names of her children. 'Angel and Noah,' she said and as she did tears welled up again in her tired looking eyes. I gently encouraged her to talk and she told me that she had come to the UK a few years ago to work as a nurse. It had not been an easy decision as it meant leaving her two children – Angel aged nine and Noah aged five – in her mother's care. She had hoped to be able to support her family better that way and secure a better future for them. She was her only hope for her children as her husband had died five years ago.

Close to tears Pearl told me that she travelled back as often as she could to see her children but on her last trip home something terrible had happened. While out shopping with Noah and Angel at a local market she had been distracted for a few moments by an argument that turned into a fist fight between two stallholders. When she looked around to check her children were okay they had vanished. At first she thought they were playing a prank on her but when she couldn't find them she started to get really anxious. There was no sign of them anywhere. No one in the market saw them leave or even remembered seeing them at all. Panic stricken she searched the local area frantically for two days but to no avail.

When I asked Pearl whether the police had been a help to her she began to cry even harder and told me they hadn't been very helpful at all. They had refused to search the area and said that a lot of children go missing or run away and they couldn't possibly chase after them all. Looking into Pearl's eyes I saw how deeply pain and fear were cutting into her. There was no question about it I had to help, if I could.

I told Pearl I would see her at her home next week; I'd have liked to have seen her sooner but my schedule wouldn't allow me. A time and day was set and I took note of her address.

I returned home feeling very anxious and praying that I would be able to shed some light on the strange disappearance. The 'couldn't care less' reaction of the police to Pearl's trauma played on my mind. It seemed very odd. Why had they been so unwilling to get involved in the case?

Falling deeper and deeper

All this happened during a very busy work period for me. I had been working flat out giving private one-to-one sittings and public demonstrations all over the country so it wasn't until two days before my next meeting with Pearl, that I managed to get a chance to work on the case properly. Before our next meeting I had asked Pearl to send me as soon as possible the following:

- The most recent drawing or painting they had made (in this case she sent me a colouring-in book of Noah's and a beautiful painting of a red and yellow butterfly that Angel had made).

- A CD or tape of music either or both children had enjoyed (a very worn and scratched Westlife CD was produced).

Together with the two photographs of the children I was ready to work.

I went to my workroom and started by listening to the CD. I'm not really a fan of Westlife but listening to the haunting and touching lyrics of 'Flying without Wings' it was absolutely impossible not to feel sad thinking about the children. Were they still alive? Were they alone and hungry? They were so young to be torn away from their mother, especially as they had never really known their father.

After listening to the music I sat down at my desk and laid the children's artwork out in front of me. Still feeling intensely emotional after listening to the music I placed my hands upon the brightly coloured images before me. As my fingers traced over the picture I began to feel the energy of a rather tall thickset man in his early thirties, he came so close the hairs on the back of my neck stood up on end. The air around me began to cool and as if he had leaned forward placing his face next to mine I heard him whisper, 'Help them. Help them. You must help them.' The words were so clear; as though they had been spoken by someone in the same room as me and at one point I turned round to check no one was there but, of course, no one was. I gathered my thoughts and closed my eyes and allowed myself to fall deeper and deeper into a trance like state. I surrendered to the spirits and opened myself to them.

I began to breathe deeply to calm and centre myself. In my mind I asked the spirit to tell me who he was but I heard nothing. Instead I received a powerful image of a young, tall man standing before me with his eyes closed. I 'knew' instinctively his name was Sammy or Samuel, then in my left ear I heard the name Samuel being called – he was showing himself to me. He was drawing me into his world.

I often see, hear, feel and sense things from the spirits but every now and again they take me on a journey in my mind to help me work with them in a clearer more powerful way. And this was happening right now. I felt myself falling deeper and deeper into the trance. Trances are fascinating experiences for me where past and present can meet with such force that they actually merge with one another in my mind and become one event that is neither past nor present but simply now. The visions I experience in trance can easily resemble spirit visits but they are unique in that the images are not coming from the other side nor are they from the earth. They are from another time and place and typically occur when a profoundly emotional telepathic empathy is established between me to another time or place. There was no doubt that my empathy for Pearl was strong and this emotional attachment was pulling me towards another time and another place.

The room I was sitting in disappeared and I found myself in another world, where past and present had merged. My heart started to pound as I realised this was happening. Time seemed to stand still and I became aware of the sensation of falling. It seemed as if the world was going crazy with anger and panic. I was running and running for my life. I heard the roar of a car engine and then I saw a beaten up old van hurtle around the corner of a dimly lit street. Bright, burning colours of red and orange surrounded me. Behind me I sensed the sound of gunshots. I heard angry shouts and screams and felt sweat trickle down my face. I felt pain. At this point I asked my guides to help me work through this traumatic memory as it was affecting my physical body too much. The guides listened and realising it was difficult for me took it away and the scene began to replay again in my mind but this time I was not part of the scene but a silent witness.

As if being catapulted forward in time I found myself watching three men place a man's lifeless body into a recently dug grave. I was in doubt that I had been at the scene of a murder and that the man lying dead before me – the man whose experience I had entered into during my trance – was Samuel.

As soon as I realised that the dead man in my vision was Samuel the images vanished and the trance was over. I opened my eyes and my hands were still on the children's artwork. I grabbed a pen and began to scribble down as fast as I could all I had seen and felt. I had no idea what I had sensed or how on earth it might all link in with Pearl and the missing children but I knew it was important and I didn't want to forget a thing.

My reading with Pearl
Two days later I travelled to Brixton, south London to meet with Pearl. She greeted me eagerly and showed me into her sitting room. I glanced at the many

pictures of Angel and Noah and sensed the unbreakable bond of love between mother and child.

We sat down and I told Pearl all about my vision and what I had seen so far concerning her children. Pearl listened with her mouth and eyes wide open. 'My husband was Samuel,' she cried out. 'He was murdered five years ago. His body wasn't found for months after. At first everyone suspected me,' she continued, 'but that's unthinkable. I loved my husband. I did not, could not kill him or kill anyone for that matter.'

I wasn't sure what to say as I was as shocked as Pearl so I simply assured her that Samuel was alive in the spirit world. I told her that his presence in my vision clearly demonstrated that he loved her still and wanted to connect with her and help her in her search.

I asked Pearl to give me some items of her children's clothing to help me to tune into their energy. She gave me a pair of Noah's trainers and placed a pink tracksuit top on my lap that belonged to Angel. As I played with the laces of the trainers and stroked the tracksuit top with absolute certainty I knew that the children were still alive. They were not yet in spirit.

'Noah and Angel are alive. They are together and being kept by someone they know.'

'Oh my God! Oh my God!' Pearl shouted. 'How are they? Are they okay?'

It was hard for me to tell Pearl that I sensed they were in distress. They were sad and crying and very,

very scared and I knew that telling this would cause her even more pain so I put this to her as sensitively as I could, but I am a messenger of truth and Pearl deserved to know what I was sensing.

Pearl sobbed and gently rocked herself backwards and forward as if to comfort herself. I prayed to the spirits to give me more. I wanted more information from them to help Pearl and they answered my prayer and gave me more. I saw Samuel appear next to Pearl. Then he looked at me with his piercing eyes and told me to tell her about a blue parrot. I've learned by now that however ridiculous the messages may seem from the spirits they are always given for a reason. A blue parrot may mean nothing to me but perhaps Pearl would understand.

'Look for the blue parrot. Does that mean anything to you? Samuel wants you to look for the blue parrot.'

'The blue parrot,' Pearl repeated slowly. 'I don't understand.'

'You've got to think, really think,' I urged. 'This is important. Samuel is telling me about a blue parrot. He's waving his hands about.'

Pearl bit her lip and chewed her fingers. Then her eyes lit up. 'Samuel's father had one. He had a blue parrot.'

'I can see a small house. I can see lots of trees. I can see a swing in the garden. Does this mean anything to you?'

Pearl rubbed her face and shook her head.

'Samuel thinks this place is important. He also says that the police know more than they are saying.'

'I don't know what you mean.'

'I'm not sure either but I can't help feeling that they do.'

'What do they know? What do they know?' Pearl asked anxiously.

'Darling, do you know a policeman?'

'Yes,' cried Pearl jumping up and sitting down again. 'Samuel's brother was and still is a policeman.'

'Does his name begin with a J?'

'My God! Yes, his name is Jacob.'

'Samuel is telling me that Jacob thinks you had something to do with his murder.'

'You're right. Jacob thinks I killed Samuel but I had never, could never. Samuel was my life, the father of my children. I loved him. I love him.' Pearl cried.

'Samuel is worried about Jacob. He says Jacob feels very angry, he wants to hurt you.'

'He has before, once he attacked me. I was terrified,' replied Pearl shaking.

'I am being shown your children in Nigeria. I can see them hugging each other tightly and watching Jacob. I feel the children are with him. You need to find them and you need to go soon, very soon. They aren't safe.'

'Why? Why?' screamed Pearl. 'Why would he take them? He was never interested in them when Samuel was alive.'

'He wants to punish you.'

'I loved Samuel. I would not have hurt him.'

'I know that because I have seen the three men who killed him.'

I couldn't believe it. I had never had a spirit come across to me so vividly and with such a specific message and purpose. It was difficult to contain my excitement and to let Samuel go but I realised time was of the essence and Pearl needed to get back to Nigeria before anything happened to her children. I finished the session and urged Pearl to take action. She promised to call me if there was any news.

The blue parrot

I called Pearl the next day and the next but there was never an answer. My work commitments kept me busy but as the days passed I kept thinking about her and every time I did I prayed that the spirits would lead her to her children. Three weeks later I finally got the phone call I had been hoping for.

One evening as I was getting ready for bed the phone rang. It was Pearl. She told me that after our meeting she had immediately booked a flight back home to Nigeria. When she arrived home she told her family what had been revealed in her reading with me and how it was possible that Jacob had the children. She asked her brothers to help her find her children and they agreed immediately. The next morning Pearl and her brothers went to Samuel's family and asked to speak to Jacob. Jacob's brothers refused even to open the door. They told Pearl they would not help and did not want to see or speak to her again.

In frustration Pearl and her brothers went to the police station where Jacob worked and she was told that he had left his job a month ago. Pearl was feeling so desperate for clues that she asked her brothers to offer some policemen a bribe to tell them where Jacob may have gone but no one was willing to take the bribe.

Pearl went on to say that after her visit to the police station she was at her lowest ebb. Returning to her family home she went to bed that evening exhausted and drained. She lay down on her bed and prayed to God for help as she was at the point of giving up her search. Then just as she was about to drift off into sleep the image of the blue parrot I had mentioned in the reading popped into her mind. At first she dismissed the thought, but so clear was the memory in her mind and so persistently did it come to mind that she knew it had to be something very important. It wasn't until the next morning when she woke with a heavy head that she realised why it was so important. She remembered that Samuel had once told her that his late father had kept a blue parrot for many years at the end of his life. The parrot had been his pride and joy. Although she had never visited her late father-in-law's house, as he had died before her marriage, she remembered that Samuel had told her he lived in a village approximately forty miles away.

With all other possibilities exhausted and the police unwilling to help or clearly covering up for Jacob, Pearl told me that she knocked on her neighbour's doors in the hope that someone knew the village where her father-in-law had lived. Fortunately, an old family friend did and Pearl travelled there with her brothers that very morning. Once there Pearl stood in the market with photographs of her children displayed on a board and asked everyone and anyone who passed by if they had seen her children. After four hours she finally stuck lucky when a middle-aged lady said she thought she had seen them before. The lady directed Pearl and her brothers to a smallish house surrounded by trees in its garden at the edge of the village.

Breathlessly, Pearl told me that as she approached the house she heard shouting inside, then she saw her children in the far corner of the garden, they were crouching behind a couple of large oil barrels that stood tall enough to conceal them. They were holding on to each other with their heads down as if they were trying to shut out the argument inside the house. The light was fading and without hesitation Pearl and her brothers seized their chance and ran into the garden, grabbed the children, bundled them into the car and sped away as fast as they could.

Pearl explained that it was all a bit of a blur as her heart was pounding with joy and her children were climbing all over her with relief and excitement at seeing their mother again but as she turned back to look at the house she saw Jacob running behind them, a club in his hand.

My knees felt weak when I heard Pearl tell me the happy news and I sat down on the floor with relief.

'You led me to my babies – thank you from the bottom of my heart. Thank you.'

'It wasn't me, Pearl,' I replied, 'it was Samuel. He led you to your children.'

Pearl sighed. 'I know he made it to the other side now but is he okay? Is he happy? Is he at peace or seeking revenge? Is he angry?'

Pearl had asked me a question I have heard so many times from grieving relatives, especially those who have lost them in tragic or violent circumstances, such as murder. I didn't mind repeating the same answer to Pearl that I repeat to everyone else. 'Anger, revenge, hurt, unhappiness, guilt and all other kinds of negativity are earthly not spirit experiences.'

I really do understand how hard it must be to imagine when we are in the grip of our own pain and suffering over the loss of someone we love that they are not in pain too. But if you never believe another thing I tell you I ask you to believe this, it's our pain, our anger, our hurt that we are projecting onto them. They are whole, happy, healthy, loving and fulfilled again in spirit looking forward to seeing us again but in the meantime there is plenty of spiritual experiences for them to enjoy with the prospect of eternity and perhaps other incarnations on earth to reflect on or look forward to. They understand life and spirit perfectly, just as we will when we meet them there.

Today Pearl keeps in touch with me and updates me on her children. They are safe and sound and remarkably unaffected by their traumatic experience. Pearl no longer lives or works in England and she has asked me not to disclose where she lives with her children now.

The bonds of love

I feel honoured to have been involved with this case as it is a very special one indeed. A mother reunited with her children by the love of her departed husband and the power of spirit and by her willingness to listen to her intuition concerning an obscure piece of information about 'a blue parrot'.

This case demonstrates my belief that loved ones and spirit guides visit us over and over again from the other side in various ways; it's not just something that happens to psychics and mediums. Yes, I had a vision of Samuel but it was Pearl who picked up on the significance of the blue parrot and it was Pearl who rescued her children. Pearl's courage and persistence makes it clear that I am not doing my work by myself. I know that there are spiritual beings, unseen and unknown who help me and by helping me they help others grow in spirit.

Above all though this case is truly special because it shows just how strong the bonds of love we create on earth can be and how they don't die but live on as we journey to the afterlife. It offers proof that love is the strongest force in the universe and so far reaching that it transcends death itself. The bonds of love, once created, always continue.

For me love is the force and the energy of the universe. In this instance the focus was on the love between a husband and wife and the love of a mother for her children and how that love binds them together but love has no limitations and no one love is superior to another. Each time you say or do a kind thing, help someone, say a prayer, offer your friendship or trust your heart you are living the divine principle of love. You begin to see the universe through loving eyes and feel the joy in everyone and everything. And when you start to do that wonderful things can and do happen because you are bringing spirit, or as some like to call it heaven, to earth.

4

A DOG'S TAIL

A great deal of the satisfaction I get from the work I do is revealed by the strength of the love that shines through in my readings among people and this is how I looked at things until the day I received a phone call from Trudy.

MY EARLY MORNING WAKE UP CALL!

It was 5.20 a.m. and the phone in my office across the landing was ringing and ringing. I yawned, put my head under the pillow and lay in my warm bed for a while hoping the ringing would stop, but it didn't. Clearly someone wanted to get in touch urgently so I crawled out of bed, stumbled around for a while trying and failing to find my dressing gown, headed into my office and picked up the phone. As I lifted the receiver and placed it to my ear, I heard a lady crying.

'Who is it? Hello?' I said.

The sobbing continued but this time it was broken up by apologies for waking me so early in the morning. The lady's distress and the sincerity of her apologies touched me. I tried not to sound annoyed but this wasn't easy as it had been a late night the night before and my eyes were closing. So I stood in my office, wearing a pair of baggy bed shorts, listening to this lady crying, telling her it really was okay to wake me at the crack of dawn and at the same time wondering if it was too late to change vocations.

After a few more minutes of tears and apologies I got impatient and asked her to call me again after 9 a.m. when I would be in a more fit state but she said she was desperate. She needed my help right now. I was just about to say that wasn't possible when my dog Archie came up to me wagging his tail with enthusiasm. I could tell he was happy to see me awake this early. Archie's affectionate energy as he pressed his body against my legs gave me the boost I needed to keep my eyes open. I settled down on the floor with Archie on my lap and listened to what I knew would be a fairly long call. I asked the distressed lady to take a deep breath and then to tell me her name and to explain why she wanted my help. The lady sighed with relief and introduced herself as Trudy. She was thirty-seven and lived in a small village on the Essex/Suffolk borders.

Trudy's story

Trudy told me that she was passionate about dogs. I told her that I was too and felt happy that we were establishing common ground so early in the conversation. She then went on to explain that having no children of her own, no close family and no relationship for the last three years she had spent a lot of time with her gorgeous Staffordshire terrier, Harry. She described Harry as a perfect gentleman and admitted that he had helped her get through some very hard times. She loved her dog with all her heart and he was allowed to sleep not just on her bed but in it. He went with her everywhere and holidays abroad were no longer an option because she didn't want to leave him in kennels. Instead, holidays were spent camping in the Lake District or in a family cottage in Devon, anywhere where they could holiday together. Harry always walked at Trudy's side wherever they went – be it shopping or running in the park – he was her constant companion.

Trudy told me Harry was five years old and white and brindle in colour. He always wore a black leather collar with silver studs and even though he rarely left Trudy's side he also had a dog tag. As Trudy described Harry I could sense the incredible love she had for her dog but then she started to tell me what had happened yesterday and I could hear her voice breaking up with emotion again.

Trudy explained that she was enjoying a typical Sunday afternoon, watching television, dozing by the fire and generally relaxing at home when Harry began to bark. At first she thought he'd heard a cat outside and told him to settle down but he continued to make a fuss so she decided he probably needed some fresh air and a run around in the garden. She opened the back door and let him out, smiling as he raced towards the back of the garden. Trudy told me her garden was narrow and long, so long that it was divided into two sections and separated in the middle by bushes and flowers. The first half of the garden was the more formal part but the back part was less well cared for and had long grass, a few fruit trees and a forgotten attempt at a vegetable plot. Harry loved the back part of the garden and thinking he was probably after the squirrels or birds there Trudy thought nothing of him disappearing into it. She shut the door and went back to watching the television.

'Harry always lets himself in,' Trudy told me next. 'I know it sounds odd, but that's the way we have always done things. I let him out and if he wants to come back in, he stands on his back legs and pulls the handle down with his front paws. He's a really clever dog. He never usually stays out on his own for long so when he hadn't come in after fifteen minutes or so, I went out to call him.'

To cut a long story short, Trudy told me that when she went out to call Harry he was nowhere to be seen.

She searched her garden and her house but there was no sign of him anywhere. She called her friends to ask them to help her look for him, knocked on the doors of neighbours to ask if they had seen him but nothing. Nobody had seen him or had any idea where he might be or what might have happened to him. It was even a mystery how he could have escaped from the garden as there were no gaps in the fence or any visible signs of how he could have got out. The fence on the right overlooked farmland and was a good four and a half foot high. Harry wouldn't have been able to jump that and even if he had, why wasn't he on the other side barking to be let back in?

Gulping back tears, Trudy explained that she had walked the streets most of Sunday night calling out his name. She returned home at midnight in a terrible state, imagining the worst possible scenarios. Perhaps Harry had been dog napped or was lying dead in a road somewhere? She tried calling the police but they simply took down details and told her he would probably turn up in a day or so. Not knowing who to turn to and feeling desperate Trudy told me that my name suddenly came into her mind. She had seen me demonstrate at a clairvoyance evening in Ipswich a year or two ago and apparently I had given her my card when she had asked about the possibility of a private consultation.

'I turned the house upside down, looking for that card,' she said. 'It took me hours to find it but when

I eventually did I called your number immediately. I haven't had any sleep myself and had lost sense of time. It was only when I called you and spoke to you that I realised what the time was and that I had woken you really early. I'm really, really sorry but I don't know who else could help me.'

I listened to everything Trudy had to say and felt deeply sorry for her but I wasn't sure how I could help as normally I work to bring people together not people and animals. I was just about to tell her to stay strong, get some flyers with Harry's picture printed and to call the local police station again when Archie, my dog, jumped off my lap and turned to face me, wagging his tail and barking. Now, I'm not saying that Archie is a wonder dog with developed psychic powers or anything and it could easily have been coincidence but jumping up so suddenly like that stopped me dead in my tracks. I looked at his pleading eyes and knew I had to help Trudy. I've always believed that animals have souls the same as humans and they have such a great capacity for love and devotion that they can change and heal our lives if we let them. Perhaps it was time to put my belief about animals to the test.

So, after giving Archie a stroke I promised Trudy I'd try to help. I told her that I hadn't worked with animals before but this was as good a time as any to start. I said I'd do my best and we should speak again in a few hours and told her to be strong. In the meantime I began to prepare myself for the worst as I realised the contact I might make with Harry could be in the spirit world.

Regarding Harry

After speaking to Trudy I went back to bed. It was still only six o'clock in the morning and I knew I'd feel and work better with a couple of hours more sleep. Archie came with me. I don't normally let him sleep in my bed but this time I did. We cuddled up and I fell asleep listening to the sound of his breathing. As sleep swept over me like a dark, comforting and warm blanket I began to dream. In my dream I was standing in a beautiful garden surrounded by trees and colourful flowers. The sun was shining and the birds were singing. It really was a beautiful day but then it began to rain. I ran around trying to find shelter but couldn't. My legs felt heavy and clumsy and I started to panic. I tried to call out but no words came out. Someone was calling me – calling my name – over and over and over again but they weren't calling my name they were calling Harry, Harry, Harry.

As soon as I realised that the voice wasn't calling out for me but for Harry, Trudy's missing dog, I woke up with a start. I glanced at my alarm clock and it was nearly nine o'clock. I had overslept. Without hesitation and still in my baggy bed shorts I went back into my office and called Trudy. She picked up the phone almost straight away. 'Yes,' she said. I told her it was me and asked her to take a deep breath and sit down.

'Harry hasn't run away or escaped, he has been stolen. He's alive but in danger.' The words came out of my mouth without me thinking about what I was saying. This sometimes happens to me and when it does, believe me, what I say can often come as much as a shock to me as it is to the person that I am speaking to. I hadn't even realised when I picked up the phone that I was going to tell Trudy that Harry was alive but in danger until I heard myself saying it.

Trudy started to panic and it took a while to calm her down. I told her about my dream and more importantly how the dream had made me feel. In my dream I had heard Harry's name being called out but it wasn't like ordinary, physical hearing it was so much more multifaceted than that. I had sensed Harry's panic as his name had been called and his desire to be reunited to Trudy and I knew that what I had sensed was very much an earth bound emotion. Harry was not yet in spirit. He was alive of that I was sure. Where he was and why he had been taken, however, was still unknown. I told Trudy that it was a mystery I would like to try and help her solve. Fortunately Trudy lived fairly close to me and I arranged to visit her later that day.

My reading with Trudy

Just before lunch I knocked at Trudy's door, no longer in my baggy bed shorts, you'll be pleased to hear, but in a warm pair of trousers and a jacket. Trudy had long curly red hair and was wearing a T-shirt with 'love me love my dog' on the front. Her eyes were red with crying. We sat in her front room, a room that reminded me of my nan's best room, only used on special days and Sundays. She offered me a cup of tea and I gratefully accepted.

I began by asking to see some photographs of Harry. I needed them to tune into Harry's energy and to encourage communication with him. Trudy handed me a huge pile of photos, there must have been hundreds, but after flicking through them I only selected three; ones that just had Harry in them and no one else. I laid the photographs out on the large wooden table in front of me in the shape of a triangle; two at the top and one at the bottom. Placing my hands either side of the bottom image I stared long and hard into Harry's face and as I did I immediately started to receive information about him.

'I feel that when you first bought Harry he wasn't your first choice. You wanted a bitch.'

Trudy smiled for the first time. 'Yes, that's right. I actually chose his sister first. I wasn't keen on having a boy; I was really going off men at the time but at the last moment the breeder decided to keep the bitch. Harry was the one puppy left. He looked so alone. I fell in love with him on the spot and took him home. It was the best decision I ever made.'

'I get the feeling that he recently had an injury of some sort; I'm feeling as if he lost a nail on his front left paw.'

'That's true,' said Trudy. 'About two weeks ago he lost a whole nail from his left front paw when we were walking in the woods.'

Feeling happy that I had established contact with Harry and was receiving good information from his photographs I tried to turn my attention to the more serious issue of where he was now. I closed my eyes and asked Harry to tell me where he was and how we could help. All sorts of emotions filled my mind and although I didn't see any visual images I felt a great deal.

'I'm sensing that Harry knows the people that have taken him. I'm sensing a man and a woman and they are married or are partners.'

'I'm a single girl, I don't really know any couples,' replied a puzzled looking Trudy.

'Let me see if I can get more details. The man is about forty to forty-three and she is younger; maybe thirty-six.'

'I can think of quite a few couples who would fit that description; not friends but people I bump into at work or in the park but I don't think any of them would be interested in Harry.'

While Trudy was thinking and talking it seemed as

if the photographs on the table in front of me were getting larger. A soft light surrounded the photograph on the top left hand side. It was calling me to concentrate on it and as I did some visual images finally came to me.

'Trudy, I can see a man with a moustache. The moustache is dark. He looks like he may have served in the army at one time or other.'

'Not my ex!' Trudy shouted. 'He's got a moustache and he was in the army, but he is single.'

'And who is Michael?'

'That's my ex.'

I asked for a photo of Michael and Trudy went to find one. She took quite a long time and when she returned she looked a little embarrassed.

'It's the only one I haven't burned or thrown away. I don't really know why I bothered to keep this one. I'm glad I did though and I hope it helps you.'

Trudy handed me the photograph of Michael. I took it and immediately realised that the man in the photograph was the man I'd seen earlier in my vision. As I looked into Michael's eyes in the photo something seemed obvious to me that had not seemed obvious before. 'He never liked Harry did he? He pretended to but he was often unkind to him. I think he was jealous and thought you loved Harry more than him.'

Trudy buried her face in her hands and started to cry. 'That's the reason why I left him. Well one of them anyway. He was jealous and controlling. I saw him kick Harry once in a temper. It's one thing him hitting me but another hurting my dog.'

The back of my hand started to tingle and burn as Trudy talked about her bitter and sometimes violent relationship with Michael. 'I feel I've got a burn on the back of my hand, like a cigarette burn.'

Trudy showed me a small scar on the back of her hand. 'That's what he did to me the week before I left. He was vile. I don't know why I stayed with him so long and if it wasn't for Harry I don't know what I would have done. It was Harry who gave me the courage to leave him. I couldn't bear to see him hurt Harry.'

I could sense that we were getting close to the truth so I closed my eyes and focused very hard. In my mind I could hear Harry barking and the noise seemed to be coming from the garden. I asked Trudy if we could go outside and explained that I needed to make a link with the last place Harry was seen to see if I could pick up his trail.

I wandered up and down the garden, spotting all the little paths Harry had made for himself and the toys, bones and chews he had left behind him. I bent down and picked up a half chewed plastic pig and held it in my hands tightly. All at once I saw Harry with a rope tied around his neck. I feared the worst but then realised it wasn't strangling him but was being used to tether him. I saw that he was outside in what looked like a forest. Trudy listened carefully as I explained what I had seen to her. Then a peculiar thing happened to me; the ground around me suddenly filled with bluebells. I wasn't at all sure what to make of this so decided not to mention the bluebells to Trudy.

In my head I heard Harry barking again and I followed the direction of the sound. It was calling me towards the fence at the side of the garden, which looked across the farmland. I touched the fence and as I did I saw in my mind the whole thing. The man with the moustache – Michael – had jumped over the fence, put a rope around Harry's neck, picked him up and handed him to a woman on the other side. I saw the two of them running away with Harry in my mind. A moment later I was aware of them putting Harry into the back of a small blue car and speeding off. They were laughing. Harry was whining. I felt Harry's thoughts at this point and started to cry.

Hastily brushing away my tears so as not to upset Trudy further I heard myself saying to her, 'they went that way' and pointing in the direction of the main road out of the village.

Lost and found

Without a moment's hesitation Trudy and I jumped into her car. We had no idea where we were going to go and I know this sounds mad but I closed my eyes and directed her to where I felt Harry was calling. Trudy headed out of the village and each time we got to a junction I'd feel the way to go. Twenty minutes later we found ourselves at a dead end. We had driven up a country path. Trudy looked at me as though she was losing faith in me, although she never said so and to be honest I was wondering at this stage if I'd led her to the wrong place. We both got out of the car and looked around. We were in the middle of nowhere.

Feeling disappointed for Trudy and not knowing what else to do I pulled a pendulum out of my pocket. Dowsing with a pendulum is a technique I sometimes use when I feel I've reached a dead end in my investigations and when my emotions are running high and making it difficult for me to see clearly. I believe all things – living and inanimate – have an energy force and when I'm feeling anxious the energy of a lost person – or in this case Harry – can find it hard to get through to me. It can be easier for their energy to influence an inanimate and more objective object like a pendulum and force it to move one way to indicate yes or the other way to indicate no.

I asked the pendulum to indicate whether or not we would find Harry today and the response was positive. I then asked if Harry was nearby and the response was again positive. Finally, I asked if we were right to explore the area and the pendulum's positive response was encouraging.

Feeling a little more confident, I asked Trudy to wait in the car while I had a look around. She looked pale and fragile and to be honest, although the pendulum had indicated that we could find Harry, I had no idea if he was alive or what state he would be in if I found him. I wanted to spare Trudy any more trauma so I walked out alone into the fields in front of me, my eyes lifted to the sky as if looking for some kind of inspiration. I asked the spirits in the other world to guide me and they responded by telling me as they often do to follow my instincts. I looked back down to the earth and started to walk and walk and walk. I don't know how long I walked but it must have been for at least half an hour.

I just followed my instincts and walked across field after field until I came to a patch of dense trees. My gut told me to keep going even though it was difficult to walk and I wasn't even wearing proper walking shoes or boots. I walked deeper and deeper into the trees until all around me I could see nothing but trees; I was lost. I began to feel angry with myself and questioned my actions; 'stupid, I'm stupid, how on earth could I for one moment really think, I could . . . .'

Then I heard the most wonderful of sounds; a dog barking. I followed the barking and started to call 'Harry, Harry'. I saw him, in a clearing in the trees surrounded by bluebells! Wide eyed he seemed to smile at me like I was an old friend. I couldn't believe I had found him. My heart was racing with excitement and tears were rolling down my face as I bent down and kissed him. Harry licked me and wagged his tail. I cuddled him and he felt cold and damp. 'Good boy, good boy', I said and as I did I noticed he had been tied to a tree with a rope around his neck.

I knew at once that he had been left there to die. Left by a man who for some twisted reason was so full of bitterness towards his ex-girlfriend that he thought he had the right to take away the one thing she loved most in the world.

Puppy love

Trudy and Harry were of course reunited and although I've witnessed many emotional reunions in my time this was one of the sweetest and most poignant. The last I heard there had been no sight of her ex; no doubt he thought he had had his revenge and was content with that. He didn't, of course, consider that the link of love between Trudy and her dog was so strong that it had allowed me to use my psychic senses to bring them back together again.

The love between an animal and its owner can be just as strong and powerful as the love between two people and in this case it was the magnet that reunited a woman with her beloved pet. I'm often asked if pets possess innate psychic ability. We've all heard amazing stories of animals sensing danger, responding to their environment or travelling incredible distances to be reunited with their owners. I truly believe pets are psychic and super-sensitive, although perhaps not all of them – only a select few have developed the 'gift' just the same as humans. I also believe that the key to developing their sensitivity is the bond of love they create with their owners. Animals can feel and sense emotions just the way that we do and the stronger the bonds of love and respect between you and your pet the more likely they are to respond and connect to you.

The bonds of love, no matter with whom, are not just powerful and unbreakable in this life, they are also powerful and unbreakable in the next. Another question I'm also often asked regarding pets is do they survive death as we do, and my answer is a resounding yes. They go to the same spirit world we do and are met by humans they had a rapport with on earth. If they had no experience of humans they are met by people who adored animals when on earth. I also believe animals who have passed may from time to time remember the kindness and love they received on earth and come back to sit in the same spot or chair or simply to watch over and protect you. That's why if you have lost a beloved pet there may be times when you sense or feel them still around you.

My message is simple: never take animals, or any living creature for that matter, for granted.

5

A DAUGHTER'S JOURNEY FROM LOSS TO LOVE

Even though it was a few years ago I remember the case of May and her daughter Pauline clearly as it was a particularly intense and difficult one for me. My work as a psychic medium was going from strength to strength and I felt I had a far greater affinity with the spirits than before and it was helping me unravel secrets or mysteries from the past or to communicate messages from the other world. I was confident of my abilities and the messages my guides were sending me but in my reading for May I lost my confidence completely. I'd had my moments in the past when I wasn't sure of myself but never to the extent when I doubted myself and my work so strongly. Was I getting things wrong?

MY READING WITH MAY

May was my first client on a busy day of one-to-one readings. As usual I got up early that morning to prepare myself and the room I use to give my private sittings. I lit a candle and poured myself a glass of water. Then I settled down in my chair, closed my eyes and focused on my breathing to quieten my mind but this time when I closed my eyes instead of meditating I found it hard to stay awake! It had been a particularly gruesome week of filming and I was annoyed with myself for feeling so run down. I didn't want my tiredness to interfere with the quality of my readings.

The door opened and a lady in her mid to late seventies came in. She had red hair and wore a stunning emerald green scarf. She had an infectious smile and introduced herself as May. I noticed that she had a soft Irish accent and when I invited her to sit down she thanked me several times for agreeing to see her. I began to explain how I work, as I always do to my clients before a reading, and how important it is for my sitters to feel relaxed and happy to receive messages from the spirit world. May seemed more than comfortable and so I focused my thoughts on her and started the reading.

What came through first in my reading with May was the overwhelming importance of family to her. She wholeheartedly agreed when I told her that she was particularly devoted to her children; they were her life. The image of two daughters and one son came through and I told May what I was seeing. At that point May stopped nodding. 'Well, not quite. You see I actually have three daughters and one son,' she said.

I apologised to May. 'There's really nothing to apologise for,' she reassured me.

I tuned in again, a little embarrassed for making a big mistake. I refocused on May and asked the spirit world to give me something accurate, not just to help and reassure May contact with spirit was being made but also to help me. I wasn't feeling confident and wanted to be more than certain that my messages were coming from a higher source. If I was to continue with the reading it had to be accurate. Immediately, a woman who introduced herself as Mary came through and I sensed that she was May's mother. 'Your mother is here, May, and I feel her name is Mary,' I said.

'That's her name,' replied May. Realising that Mary is an extremely popular name in Ireland I knew that this wasn't good enough. I needed more detailed information. I asked the spirits to give me more and a vision of a woman in her early to mid fifties appeared in my mind. I saw her involved in a terrible accident; a car crash. 'She wasn't driving but a car killed her.' May narrowed her eyes and replied; 'My mother died when she was fifty-four. She was hit by a car when she was crossing a road.'

The more May encouraged me with her positive response the stronger the image of Mary became in my mind. 'Mary tells me she loves you very much. She often watches over you, you know, even though she says you are all grown up now. You sometimes wear her clothes don't you? She likes that.'

May smiled and gently stroked her green scarf; 'This belonged to my mother. She loved clothes. She was such a stylish beautiful lady. I wear it today for her; although it looked much better on her.'

'She says it looks stunning on you,' I replied. 'I feel she is with your father. She is talking about Pat.'

'Yes, my father's name was Patrick.'

Growing in confidence I could have gone on indefinitely offering May personal details and information about her parents. She was enjoying every moment and just as I was about to call it a day because I only had a few minutes left before my next client, Mary's voice echoed loud and clear in my mind. 'Pauline isn't hers. She isn't her daughter.' The message was so strong and so empathic it took even me by surprise. 'Who's Pauline?' I asked. May told me Pauline was her eldest daughter. 'Do you know another Pauline?' I asked as I was getting the sense that the Pauline Mary was referring to was not May's daughter but someone else's. May shook her head. 'Is Pauline definitely your daughter?' I heard myself saying several times.

May's mouth dropped open and she stared at me for what seemed a very long time before saying flatly; 'Is my mother trying to tell you something?'

'I think she is,' I replied. I didn't tell May this but I also felt that Mary and I were having a private conversation or the kind of conversation you have in hushed whispers so that nobody else can overhear.

After a few moments of silence May cleared her throat and told me that although Pauline wasn't hers she had brought her up as if she was her own and loved her more than life itself. 'Pauline is very much my daughter,' May said with moist eyes. 'I love her very much. She is as much a part of me as my other two girls and my son.'

I wanted May to feel uplifted and peaceful after her meeting with me, not upset so I apologised. May looked at me and said, 'It's not you that should say sorry. It's my mother. She promised me, she swore to me in fact, that she would never talk about this to anyone, ever.'

It would have been good to have had more time with May but I was overrunning already and had to finish the session. I told her to contact me again if she felt she needed to and reassured her that her mother loved her deeply both in this life and the next. May told me that she had got a lot out of the meeting and that she didn't feel the need to meet up again; if she felt low she would play the tape she had made of the reading. I told her that I felt my reading hadn't been as accurate or as helpful as I would have liked. May smiled and told me that I had helped her enormously and that I should never doubt my gift.

As May left the room I sat down in my chair and gave myself five minutes to gather my thoughts before my next client. Strangely I wasn't feeling tired anymore.

In fact I felt amazing, bursting with energy. I realised that the spirits were most definitely with me and I shouldn't ever have doubted them. I thanked May in my heart for believing in me and was convinced that I would hear from her again but I had no idea where or when.

MY MEETING WITH PAULINE

About six or seven months later I got a phone call from a woman, early one Tuesday morning. 'Hello, you don't know me, but my mother had a reading with you earlier in the year. She recently passed away but just before she died she told me to listen to a tape recording of the reading she had with you.' I listened, not sure at all where this was leading but then everything fell into place when she told me that her name was Pauline and that she would like my help.

Without hesitation I agreed to meet with her the following week and when we met she explained to me that her mother had been suffering for many years with cancer and had only died two weeks before. 'Before mum died,' Pauline said sadly, 'she said she wanted to tell me something about a tape. I didn't have a chance to listen to it as she went down rapidly and my life stood still until she passed. I found the tape when I was clearing out her stuff and listened to it.'

Pauline played the tape to me and we listened together. I needed to refresh my memory as although I remembered some of it I often have no recollection of the details of readings I've given. As I heard myself talking to May I was able to link back into the thoughts, images and feelings I had received previously. I was sad to hear that she had passed as I had hoped to meet with her again in this life but I knew that she was being well cared for in spirit.

Pauline asked what she should do with the information I had revealed. She explained that if her mum was not her birth mum then, although she loved May dearly, a part of her needed to know who she was and why she was given up for adoption.

I thought about the consequences of what had come through from the other world in my reading with May and felt more than a little responsible. But then I realised that if May had never wanted Pauline to know she could have simply destroyed the tape after the sitting and never mentioned it to a living soul. Yet she had chosen to tell Pauline about the tape before she died and this had prompted Pauline to contact me and ask for help. A sense of urgency came over me and I decided to give Pauline a reading right there.

Within moments an image of May with her fabulous warm smile came into my mind. I told Pauline that May was with her and wanted her to know that she loved her very much; just as much as her other three children. Pauline smiled with tears in her eyes saying, 'I know she does. I've always known that.'

'She's sorry for not explaining things to you before,' I said.

'Please tell her I love her and will always love her but I need to know the truth,' Pauline replied.

As soon as I heard Pauline tell me how much she needed to know the truth I felt as if I was thrown into another world; a world I simply didn't understand and where there were so many mysteries to uncover. I felt overcome with emotion and holding back the tears I saw a scene from the past play itself out in front of me.

In my vision I saw a very young couple kissing passionately by a farmer's gate. The girl had very long blonde hair and the boy was dressed in oil stained over-alls. They looked no more than fifteen or sixteen; they were very young and very much in love. I instinctively knew that this was a scene from Southern Ireland. I was looking back to the 1950s. Suddenly the sky became overcast and the scene changed to another one. This time I saw the same young girl with blonde hair crying and wringing her hands. She was talking to an older man and he felt like her father. Next to the young girl trying to comfort her I saw May as a young woman in her mid twenties. In a flash the image melted and changed again. Now I was seeing May holding a newborn baby girl. I felt what May was feeling and it was a mixture of love, sadness and elation.

Throughout these three visions I had been describing to Pauline all that I was seeing, sensing and feeling. I opened my eyes and leaned forward to check that Pauline was okay and saw that she was crying. I asked

Pauline if she wanted to take a break but she was keen to continue and so I leaned back in my chair and travelled back in my mind again. May was still very much with me.

'I feel that your birth mother was your mother's sister. May is telling me about a boy called Bryan. Do you know a Bryan?' I asked Pauline.

'Bryan, Bryan. No, I don't think I know anyone by that name,' Pauline said hesitantly.

'May is telling me to look on top of the wardrobe in the spare room. This is really important she really wants you to look there. She wants you to look there now.'

Pauline rushed home without wasting any time. She later told me she had looked on the top of the wardrobe in the spare room and found an old metal biscuit tin. Inside the biscuit tin there were hundreds of black and white photographs. Pauline told me that she had looked through these photographs many times and she wasn't at all sure if this is what her mother wanted her to look at. I told her that it would still be a good idea to look through them. Pauline put the kettle on and we started sorting through the photographs.

The tin was bursting and there were lots of photographs of farm animals and horses as May was from a farming family. I asked Pauline to set aside all the photographs of the people she didn't recognise. There were a few black and white photos but one she couldn't ever remember seeing before was of a group of four teenagers larking about and smiling back at the camera. The photograph was of two young couples. They were standing by an old car. One of the couples was Pauline's mother May and her father, Patrick, and the other couple was a girl with long fair hair and a boy in mechanic's overalls. On the back of the photograph written in faint handwriting were the following words: Patrick and May, Kath and Bryan, 1951.

Pauline showed me the picture at our next meeting. Instinctively, I realised that Kath and Bryan were Pauline's biological parents, but this still didn't explain why May had brought Pauline up and what became of her real parents. It was a lot for Pauline to take in but I told her that May and Kath were together in the spirit world and wanted her to know how much they both loved her. Kath also wanted Pauline to know that she was very sorry she had not been around to see Pauline grow into a beautiful woman but that she had always thought about her when she was alive and was watching over her from the other world. I told Pauline that Kath kept saying over and over again; 'my daughter, you are my daughter' and that she wanted Pauline to read a letter with a red ribbon tied around it.

Pauline had so much information to digest I decided it was time to end the session. I could sense that she felt very confused and a little betrayed by her family and that she needed time to sort things out in her head. As she left I reassured her again how much she was loved in the spirit world by both May and Kath. I asked her to keep in touch and to let me know how things worked out for her.

A tale of two mothers

Every year thousands of people are adopted or are brought up by people who are not their birth parents and for some of these people there is a burning need to know the truth. This doesn't mean that they love those who have raised them any less; it simply means they have a desire to unravel the mystery and history of their lives. In many cases finding out the truth can be painful but, as Pauline was to discover, it can also be healing.

Six weeks later Pauline called me to tell me what she had uncovered. She told me that after our reading she had questioned her brother and sisters but each of them knew absolutely nothing of the matter. They were as shocked as she was that their mother could have kept such a secret like this for so long from the people she loved dearest in the world. At this point Pauline realised that there was nothing else she could do but fly to Ireland to visit her mother's sister and brother. But when the subject was raised her aunt got very agitated and refused to say anything except 'what is in the past should stay there'. Feeling frustrated and confused by the secrecy Pauline went to see her uncle who having been pre-warned by his sister that Pauline was asking questions was also reluctant to speak. It was only when Pauline showed her uncle the photograph of Kath and Bryan with May and Patrick and started to cry that he agreed finally to tell her the truth.

Pauline's uncle told her that his youngest sister Kath got pregnant when she was just sixteen. The father was a young and foolish boy called Bryan and when he heard the news he refused to marry her and left; probably to live with relatives in England. This left Kath in a desperate position as her parents being devout Roman Catholics took the news of an unmarried pregnancy very badly indeed. Eventually, a plan was hatched. It was decided that Kath should be sent to live with her sister May who was a few years older and who had recently married and moved to a new area with her husband. Keen to spare her sister public condemnation May told her new neighbours that she was expecting a baby. To make sure everyone believed her she even placed a cushion under her clothes whenever she left the house and when Kath started to show she stayed indoors and didn't go out anymore. Pauline was born at home and on the birth certificate May and her husband's names were recorded. Soon after the birth Kath returned to live with her parents and no one ever suspected a thing. As her uncle put it, 'it wouldn't be such a scandal today about Kath getting pregnant so young but we have to remember that this was 1950's Ireland.' The story didn't end here though. Pauline's uncle told her that all seemed well for everyone but poor Kath who was broken hearted not only by her lover's betrayal but also because she had to give up her daughter. When Pauline was just five months old, Kath took her own life.

Clearly overcome with emotion as she told me her story I could feel how hard it was for Pauline to learn the truth about her life. I asked if she was okay and she nodded and said I needed to know everything. She told me that before she left her uncle he went upstairs in his home and came down after a while clutching a letter in his hand, a letter tied in a red ribbon. 'I took it trembling as I remembered what you had said in our reading,' Pauline told me. She then went on to say that the letter was from her mother, Kath, and it had been sent to her uncle shortly before she took her life. The letter was all about how much love she had for her child. The last line spoke of how she 'would have to stay strong for my little girl, the little girl I will never call my daughter.'

Pauline then thanked me for the messages I had brought to her and how it had been a life changing experience. She told me she now has a full sized photo of Kath and has placed it alongside a photo album dedicated to her mum May. She assured me that she was feeling a bit battered and bruised emotionally but okay. In fact she felt blessed telling me that not only did she have the powerful love of one mum in the spirit world she had two. 'I believe the spirit world wanted me to know that,' she said confidently. 'I feel stronger with both of them loving me up there.'

Letting go

Thankfully we live in an age when women like Kath and May would not have to go through the trauma and intrigue of disguising a pregnancy and this case is a great reminder of how far we have come. Having said that we all from time to time for one reason or another cover up our feelings or the truth with lies, but what we don't realise is that covering up is one of the greatest hurts we can inflict on ourselves and others. One of the greatest purposes of our lives is to feel; it is feelings that bring truth and change to our lives and without truth and change there can be no growth.

Pauline found out the truth of her life and it made her and her family stronger. Her mother May was also able to let go of the lies and admit the truth at the end of her life and I know it has made her stronger in spirit. How do I know? I know because a few weeks after my last chat with Pauline I went to a demonstration of mediumship. I like to do that sometimes to watch and learn from others. I never really expect something to come through for me but on this occasion it did and the medium simply told me that a May had come through and she wanted to say, 'thank you'. I smiled inwardly. Incredibly, May had chosen to thank me through someone else; perhaps to make sure that I would never doubt myself and the spirit world again.

6

THE SMELL OF PINK ROSES

Every day of our lives our bodies and minds are not only affected by the thoughts and feelings we create but also by the thoughts and feelings of those who surround us. That's why you need to pay attention not just to your own thoughts and feelings but also to the people you associate with, as we are the company we keep. It's also very important to understand that it is not just the living that can impress us with their thoughts; those in the other world can too. That's why during the day you may for no reason start thinking of a loved one who has passed over.

Most of the time I can protect myself from the wandering thoughts and emotions of others and I only let down my guard to pick up energy patterns and invite spirits in when I'm doing a reading or a public demonstration. On rare occasions, however, the thoughts and personality of someone, either in this life or the next, are so strong that my normal defences don't work. The following case is an example of how, without invitation or warning, the energy patterns and thoughts of a young girl impressed themselves upon me with such force and clarity that they were impossible to dismiss or ignore.

BRIEF ENCOUNTERS

One evening I went to bed feeling very tired but instead of nodding off the instant I hit the pillow as I normally do, I spent most of the night staring at the ceiling. Every time I managed to fall asleep I had a strange dream that woke me up with a start. Then I'd stay awake for a few hours before falling asleep and waking up again after the same dream.

In my dream I was outside at night. I was walking quickly and then out of the corner of my eye I saw a small, silver car on my left. The car stopped and someone rolled down the window as if to ask directions. I tried to run but it was as if my feet were set in concrete. I couldn't move. At this point feelings of panic and terror washed over me and I woke with a start. I must have had this same dream at least four or five times during the night. It was not only frightening but exhausting.

When morning finally came I lay in bed listening to the wind and rain outside trying to make sense of the dream. From experience I know how easy it is to forget dreams once the day begins so I scribbled down the details in my dream journal. I always have a dream journal by my bed as I believe dreams can reach beyond the boundaries of space and time and can provide messages in the form of intuitive flashes. But what was this dream trying to tell me? I didn't have a clue and decided to get up and try and interpret the images later in the day.

At the bottom of the stairs I'm used to getting a rapturous welcome from my dogs but not this morning. Instead, there was a heady scent of roses and in my mind I knew them to be pink roses. Thinking how strange this was as I don't have pink roses in my garden I walked into my dining room wondering where my dogs were. I saw them both huddled together in a corner. The scent of pink roses was stronger than ever. I called to my dogs but they didn't come over; although Archie wagged his tail and Ada started to bark. I went over to them to see why they were acting so weird and as I did I realised that they were actually both ignoring me. They were staring at something in the kitchen. I sat down with my dogs on the floor and looked in the direction they were looking. It was then that I saw her. Standing in my kitchen there was a young woman with very long hair. She was no more than twenty or so years old. She looked lost and confused. I'm not used to seeing spirits without invitation or warning and the experience startled me. My astonishment obviously startled her too as she vanished before I had a chance to ask who she was and why she was in my kitchen. As soon as she vanished the smell of pink roses vanished too and my dogs jumped on my lap in their usual enthusiastic way. I gave them a big cuddle and let them out for a run around in the garden.

What the hell! Who was she? Why was she in my kitchen? Why did I smell the roses? I thought to myself as I watched my dogs chasing each other in circles. I envied their ability to forget what they had seen, not ask questions and simply have fun. I just couldn't do that. I believe that animals can be very sensitive or psychic to changes in the atmosphere around them; often feeling and sensing things that we cannot, so I wasn't surprised that Archie and Ada had seen the girl before me.

I got dressed and had a quick breakfast and then went into my study to meditate. After my bad night I needed to calm my mind and to prepare for the day ahead but I couldn't stop thinking about the girl I had seen. Before I started my meditation I asked my guides to show me only what I needed to see. I was still feeling very confused about my dreams and my vision of the young girl looking so scared and alone. I asked my guides to show me what I could do to help her and after a few moments I heard the welcome and warm voice of Star, one of my main helpers in the spirit world. Star didn't give me any details but simply said: 'We are aware – trust us.'

Feeling reassured I breathed in and began my

morning meditation. Sometimes when I meditate I imagine in my mind's eye that I am walking on a beach. I'm looking out to a blue sea and am aware of birds flying above me calling out their morning song and praising the Great Spirit energy for all the wonders of the world. I walk along a sandy bay and then sit down and look out at the ocean, warm and gentle waves lapping at my feet. I can hear the sound of water as it reaches the shore.

Meditation helps calm and quiet my mind and allows me to connect with the universal power that surrounds and connects us all. The great majority of times thoughts, feelings and anxieties wash over me when I meditate but today felt very different. The solitude and peace of my meditation was actually making me feel more agitated. I found it hard to breathe and had to take deep breaths. Then my beach vanished and for no reason the images in my mind changed completely. Gone was the sunshine and instead I saw the light of the moon. Once again I was walking down the same street I had seen in my dream. Once again I saw the small silvery blue car but this time I saw the initials SK on its back window. I also saw a man walking towards me. He walked strangely as if he had one leg shorter than the other. I saw his face. He had dark eyes, a closely cropped beard with hints of grey, short dark brown hair and I could smell the stench of tobacco on his breath. His energy scared me so much that I jolted out of my meditation and stood up shaking my legs as if to shake off the images and the feelings I had been shown.

'What's going on, here?' I asked Star. As a worker for the spirits I rely on Star to act as a master of ceremonies and to filter images between this world and the next so that I receive information when I am ready to receive it. Star often works with me when I give readings to other people or do public demonstrations. But this was totally different. I didn't feel that Star was with me. I hadn't asked for these images and feelings and I wasn't doing a reading. First the unsettling dreams, then the girl in the kitchen and now this! I didn't like it at all and certainly didn't appreciate the intrusion into my own personal time. I knew all that I had seen was somehow connected but I just couldn't work out how. Where was Star! I was worried that he might have left me but then I felt his gentle presence beside me and he was speaking louder than usual. He told me not to feel angry or scared but to stay calm and to trust him. As he spoke, I felt instantly calmer because I would trust Star with my life. He is my friend.

Suddenly, the telephone rang in my office across the hall. I was still feeling shaky so I decided not to answer it and wait for the answer machine to click on. I listened and heard a familiar voice say; 'Tony are you there? I need to speak to you. Please pick up if you are in. I really could do with your help.' I recognised the voice immediately. Even though we hadn't spoken for at least a year, I knew it was my friend, John, from the States.

I picked the phone up and John explained that he had been asked to help trace a missing girl. While we were speaking a fax from John started to print out in front of me and I found myself looking at the face of a very pretty young woman. She had long hair and a deep dimple in her chin.

'Her parents are trying to find her,' John explained. 'She's been missing a long time. Her father is very ill and it's his dying wish to see his daughter before he dies.' John started to cough as he always does when he talks to me. I think it is a mixture of nerves and disbelief that he is actually phoning a psychic medium for advice!

I listened to what John was saying and stared at the face of the girl looking up at me.

John cleared his throat and muttered. 'Do you have any idea where we should look? Just say the word and I'll get you some details, some more photos or anything you need to help you work. They think she may have moved to Chicago because she had loads of friends there. Tony, are you still there. You've gone quiet?'

My heart was beating fast. I was feeling quite unwell and a headache was coming on. I apologised to John for my silence and told him I would definitely call him back later that morning.

My American friend

I'd first met John about seven years ago after I'd given
a demonstration at a small hall in west London and
he approached me after and asked if I had time to
have a coffee with him. He said he 'liked my style'. He
was a heavy-set man in his late forties with a strong
American accent. He seemed like a nice, genuine guy
so I agreed.

We went to a nearby café and ordered tea and coffee.
'In the demonstration,' said John as soon as the
waitress had left. 'You spoke to a man at the back of
the room and mentioned he had a friend who had
been murdered. Do you remember?'

After a demonstration working with a live audience
I usually feel a bit spaced out for a few hours so I
nodded slowly. John frowned. I think he thought I
wasn't paying attention but the message I had given
was still clear in my mind because it was so striking.
I clearly remembered having a vision during the
demonstration of a young man shot in a drive-by
shooting. 'Yes, I do remember,' I reassured him.

John looked at me for what seemed a long time. 'I
could do with help from someone like you,' he said
coughing and clearing his throat. He went on to
explain that he was a retired policeman but he loved
the job so much he couldn't leave police work
completely behind and was now working as a private
investigator helping people discover the truth or locate
missing loved ones. It's not always easy for me to trust

people, especially one claiming to be a retired police-man, and at this point I really wanted to leave without appearing too rude. Just as I was about to say I needed to leave, John's phone rang. He apologised and took the call and this gave me a chance to tune into his energy and as I did I felt nothing but sincerity, even though it was mixed with a hint of scepticism. 'That was one of my clients,' he explained when the call ended. 'Nothing I can't sort out without your help. The poor guy's business partner has done a runner with all his money.' There was a hint of a smile when he spoke and I couldn't help but smile too. I liked this guy.

Reminding myself that it was getting late I started to gather my coat and bag when John hastily took out a photo of a young boy from his pocket and handed it to me.

'What do you think? Do you think you can help?' he asked.

Something about John made me want to help him so I took the photo and looked into the boy's eyes. The room started to fade away and I saw an image of the boy on a sandy beach playing with a man he knew to be his father. Father and son were laughing and throwing a beach ball to each other. I told John what I had seen. 'Wow! So he's got him.' John replied. 'I'm working for the boy's mother. She thinks her ex-husband has abducted him and taken him to . . .' and before John could finish what he was saying I heard myself say out loud, 'Brazil. He's taken him to Brazil.' John just looked at me and smiled. 'Holy cow! Now that is impressive. That's where we believe them to be. How could you know that?'

When I interrupted John mid-sentence to tell him the boy was in Brazil with his father I wasn't trying to impress him I just wanted to help. Sometimes images and words pop into my mind and I need to say them immediately as, like dreams, they can fade from my memory very quickly unless I speak them or write them down immediately. I don't always understand what I am saying or feeling and often it confuses me, but I always try to use my gift wisely and I truly believe that the information I see or feel is revealed to me for the benefit of others.

Tears and petals

That was some time before John called me out of the blue and sent a fax asking if I could help him find this missing girl. After hanging up the phone I sat at my desk for several minutes with the fax in my hands and then from nowhere tears started to fall down my cheeks.

There have been times as an adult when I have shed the odd tear but it has been a while since I have felt as wretched as this. I cried and cried and cried some more. I don't think I'd cried like this since my beloved aunt passed away some years before. Not knowing what else to do or how to stop the crying I went into my bedroom; got into bed and pulled the covers up over my head. I stayed there for a long time feeling as if my heart was splitting at the seams.

Then I felt someone standing next to the bed. It wasn't a feeling or a vision in my mind's eye. It was like a physical presence. My heart began to beat very fast. I wasn't scared but I wasn't used to this kind of presence appearing without warning. I knew that I was alone in the house and I knew instinctively that the presence was that of the young girl I had seen in my kitchen. She was also the young girl pictured on the fax John had sent me. My eyes were sore with tears and I slowly lifted my head from under the covers. I didn't see anything but was aware again of the smell of pink roses all around me. Words started to somersault into my mind. I didn't hear them but I knew them. They were telling me that the tears I was shedding were not mine; they belonged to the young girl. The pain I was feeling was not mine. It was the young girl's. As soon as I understood that my feelings were not my own the crying stopped and the presence vanished.

I called John, straight away. 'The girl you mentioned.' I blurted out. 'She's passed over, and has been for some time. She must have known you were going to ask me for help because she has made her presence felt to me in my dreams and this morning.'

There was a long pause and a few coughs before John replied. 'Are you sure? Her mother seems to think that she is living with friends. They had some kind of argument a couple of years back and it was so bitter that they haven't spoken since.'

I took a deep breath. 'Chicago is important. She has definitely passed over and there is something not right about the way she went either. I believe she was murdered.'

'Holy cow! You're shitting me,' muttered John. 'I'll get back to you.'

A few days passed and the girl didn't come back to visit me. As the days melted into weeks I even managed to stop thinking about her completely and there were no more strange visions in my kitchen or in my dreams.

I'll see you on Sunday

About three weeks later I came home one night and switched on my computer to check my emails. Immediately I saw that one was from John. I opened it and read what he had to say. In the email he was asking for my help again. He said he needed more information from me. He wanted to know if I could tell him where the young girl died and when. He told me that her father was getting worse and was desperate to make contact with his daughter before he died. John explained that he had become very emotionally involved with this case and really wanted to help the family. With an email attachment he sent me some more photos and also said that he had sent via express delivery a vest worn by the girl a few days before she left her parents' home for the last time.

As promised the vest arrived a few days later in a brown padded envelope. Before unwrapping it I called John. Then putting him on handsfree speakerphone I tore open the envelope, took out the vest and held it to my face. Images hurtled into my mind all at once. I saw a big white house with a veranda and a small swing in the garden. I saw a pink bedroom with lots of posters on the walls and a large blue bear on the bed. I saw a large initial J.

As each scene came into view, I explained to John exactly what I was seeing.

'Wow, that's her home,' he replied, 'and I saw that bear myself when I visited the family. Not sure about the initial J though.'

Once again I was aware of the smell of flowers and those flowers were pink roses. 'I'm seeing and smelling pink roses, John. Not sure what they mean, but there are lots of them.'

Then, as if I'd suddenly jumped forward in time I saw yet again the car I had seen previously in my dreams. This time the driver was getting out and walking towards me. He was smiling and asking me to get into his car. I wanted to run away but I couldn't and as if I was hypnotised I found myself getting into the car. I saw the car driving out of town. 'He drove her out of town,' I told John. 'She knew something didn't add up with this guy. I can feel her fear at this point.'

John was coughing again, 'Why did she get into his car? Why would . . .'

Before John could finish speaking the answer to his questions came into mind. 'She got into the car because she was working as a prostitute.' The words were spoken through me. They did not come via my mind, my thoughts, but simply came out of my mouth. I felt a little startled, but continued to tell John what I was seeing and sensing.

I saw the man pull her out of his car. I saw her stumble in her high heels and fall over and then stand again. She struggled to get away from him and ran in the direction of a derelict commercial building. There were puddles of water on the floor and litter and empty cardboard boxes all around. Then I 'heard' the sound of a passing train overhead. I saw her fall again and I saw him standing over her, laughing. The smile made me shudder. It was the smile of a hunter who has found his prey. Then I saw nothing but darkness, tears and emptiness.

With John still on speakerphone I dropped the vest and picked up a pen and began to write with great urgency. The pen took on a life of its own. As if it was being manipulated by an unseen hand I wrote down: 'Tell my father I'll be waiting for him on Sunday,' and 'pink roses for mother.'

I read out what I had written to John and he coughed and mumbled a lot. 'What the hell can I do with this? Thanks for your help but not very comforting news to give to a dying father is it? Let me make some more enquiries. I'll keep you posted. Thanks again Tony, even though this isn't what I wanted to hear.' John put the phone down and I sat down feeling overwhelmed but also relieved to have seen the truth.

Four days later John called again. 'You'll never guess what, the old man died on Sunday. I didn't have the heart to tell him what you told me but do you think she will be waiting for him on the other side? Is that what you meant by see you on Sunday?'

'Yes, it must have been,' I replied. 'I'm sure she will be welcoming him with open and loving arms.'

'And that's not all of it,' said John, this time interrupting me. 'His wife told me that she has always put pink roses by her daughter's photo every week since she disappeared. I called her this morning and she also told me that before her husband died he told her he "saw" his daughter in a dream and she said she was "waiting for him". This stuff is starting to blow my mind, Tony. How on earth do you cope with it all?'

'It's what I do,' I replied.

Later that day I decided to record the case for my records. I felt the need to personalise the girl I had seen by giving her a name. I called her Jude. Although I had seen the initial J in one of my visions, I can't say I heard the name or saw it written over my head. It just felt right.

Exactly one month later I received an email from John. It read:

> Wanted to let you know that I went to Chicago and managed to track down a few friends of hers, and pow! I asked her friends if they knew if she had ever worked as a prostitute and one of them told me that she had been involved with drugs and now and again worked the streets to support her habit. I've also found out that in the same area and time she went missing a guy in a silver car had been bothering the regular girls that worked there and one girl reported being attacked by him. But so far I've come up with no body and no clues. I don't want to tell her mother, unless something concrete comes up. Oh yes, one more thing that might help. In Chicago she went by a few different names, especially when she was working the streets. She called herself Julie, Jules and Jude. You've sure been a great help Tony. I don't know how you do it but thanks and I hope we can work together again.

This case remains ongoing and if the opportunity arises to visit the States to do some investigations I may one day visit Chicago and see if I can pick up new leads.

EMBRACING NEW LIFE

This case stands out for me as it is a little different from the cases I normally work on because in this instance I never met the girl's family and didn't even know her name. Throughout I simply worked blind and had no involvement with anyone living. The only information I got was from John. All my connection was made with the girl herself in the afterlife. Also I had not asked her to contact me; she had initiated contact with me and made her presence felt first in my dreams and then in my kitchen. I haven't seen or sensed her again and, although her body has yet to be discovered, I believe she is at peace.

When a person dies suddenly or violently and leaves bewildered loved ones behind wondering what has happened to them a spirit may sometimes find it hard to accept the fact that they are effectively 'dead'. It is quite common for this type of spirit to attend their own funeral. Many times this act helps them realise they are no longer connected to the earth. Sometimes though, as was the case with Jude where no funeral was possible, a spirit may take a little longer to understand that their life on earth is over. That's why Jude's presence in my house felt almost like a physical one. Fortunately, there are advanced spiritual beings and they often choose to help those that need encouragement to fully embrace their new life in the spirit realm.

I felt honoured to have been able to help Jude relay the truth and find peace. By using me to revisit the nightmare of her death I knew that she had finally let go of the past and she no longer needed to hold on to the memories of her passing. I knew this because she had visited her dying father in her dreams after she had shown me how she died in a vision. There was no doubt in my mind that Jude had now moved out of my kitchen and into her spiritual home.

PART TWO:

INVESTIGATING THE UNEXPLAINED

Most of us have heard the expression 'having eyes in the back of your head'. In other words, knowing what's going on behind you. Well, that's what it's like for me, but rather than just seeing things that relate to the here and now I can sometimes also see things that have happened hundreds or thousands of years ago. Now, I know that sounds a little weird, but it isn't really! Our emotions leave behind impressions and these impressions stain the atmosphere they leave behind and as long as those impressions remain a psychic may be able to read and interpret them years later.

Personally, I start by giving myself a reference – perhaps a place name, a year or a situation – and then I simply 'let go'. And as long as the mystery that needs to be solved is ultimately for good then space and time can open up to me. It's like time travelling in the mind. At times I feel very little and just watch the past unravel, but at other times it's as though I've been transported back and can almost taste the very air and wander the streets of the past.

7

JACK THE RIPPER

The legend of Jack the Ripper conjures images of fog-shrouded streets, the sound of footsteps clicking loudly and menacingly on cobble stoned alleys, visions of a well-dressed fiend with evil eyes and a dark curled moustache, thin fingers and a black medical bag dangling from them.

In the history of criminology no case has haunted public imagination more than the murders of five women in the East End of London attributed to the first officially recognised serial killer of the modern era – Jack the Ripper. Although committed well over a hundred years ago these still unsolved murders have spawned countless theories, films, books, studies and documentaries. The grisly details of the infamous murders along with the mystery surrounding the killer's identity and the apparent lack of an understandable motive continue to fascinate, repel and bewilder experts, psychologists and criminologists alike. Not surprisingly, over the years the case has also attracted the attention of numerous psychics and mediums – myself included.

SETTING THE SCENE

To set the scene for this chapter let's briefly step back in time to the autumn of 1888 when the Ripper went on his rampage, killing at least five women with an escalating fury. The object of his attack it appears was not sex or murder but mutilation. His 'technique' of laying his victims down before or after he slashed their throats, then disembowelling them in a matter of a minute or two with as little blood flow as possible distinguishes him as one of the most methodical, ruthless killers to ever live. He even performed some of his gruesome murders right in the street and left his victims to be found minutes later by people or policemen passing by. This demonstrates what extreme risks he would take to fulfil his desire for killing.

The murders occurred on Friday, Saturday or Sunday nights, suggesting a man who may have had a job during regular working hours but to this day his identity has not been discovered. It was as if he vanished into thin air after each murder, disappearing as abruptly as he had arrived. How is it possible that so few clues were found? How could a man drenched in blood simply disappear? How could he escape when one-third of the police force, both undercover detectives and bobbies in uniform, were stationed in and near dozens of pubs and rooming houses, patrolling the same routes throughout the area every fifteen minutes? Did he escape through the ancient but still vast underground labyrinth of London's sewage system? Or was he himself a policeman?

These questions remain unanswered but we do know that the horrific murders sent fear throughout London, not just in the East End where they occurred. It probably didn't help anyone's peace of mind that Robert Louis Stevenson's play *Dr. Jekyll and Mr. Hyde* was playing at London's Lyceum Theatre. Unfortunately, unlike Mr. Hyde, Jack was not an uncouth monster and he certainly did not look like a murderer. He must have been charming and even respectable looking as he managed to convince women, painfully aware of the dangers of a monster in their midst, to go off with him.

All the murders took place in London's East End and Whitechapel sections. Even today, the brooding atmosphere of Victorian times still lingers in the east London neighbourhood, which has become forever identified with these notorious unsolved crimes. At the time this part of London was considered to be the dumping grounds of society. Slum buildings, lodging houses and dilapidated shops lined crooked and narrow cobblestoned streets. Traders pushing loaded carts crowded the streets by day, hawking their wares while day-workers roamed back and forth to slaughterhouses and meat markets, sometimes covered in blood. Sanitation was practically non-existent and the resulting filth and stench permeated the air hovering over the entire area.

Jack seemed well acquainted with the grim backstreets and alleyways of Whitechapel, which made it ideal territory for him to stalk his victims and then escape undetected. What would possibly lure Jack to such a place? The main attraction would appear to be the dozens of known brothels and over a thousand prostitutes – no one knows exactly how many prostitutes plied their trade because many women resorted to 'casual prostitution' once in a while to make ends meet. For Jack the Ripper prostitutes were easy prey.

Despite the dozens of books written about Jack the Ripper, books crammed with speculation about his identity and his motivation, the fact is we still don't know anything about the actual man who committed the most infamous murders in crime annals. The only thing positively known about the Ripper is who his victims were.

The exact number of victims in the Ripper's killing spree is difficult to ascertain. Up to fourteen have been pinned on him but in fact the police have only accepted five. Over time as the Ripper became a legend, they've been all but forgotten. So who were they?

Mary Ann Nicholls, née Walker, the Ripper's first official victim, was forty-three when she was murdered. At the age of nineteen she had married William

Nicholls and bore him several children but when William ran off with another woman Mary turned to drink and prostitution. At 3.30 on the morning of 31 August 1888, Police Constable John Neil walked his beat, passing by Buck's Row, just off Whitechapel. A lone gas lamp at the end of the street provided feeble light and enough shadows to hide anyone who did not wish to be seen. All was quiet, no drunken disturbances, no brawls, just a dark and narrow, filthy street winding around dilapidated hovels and slaughterhouses. Upon his return to the location ten minutes later, Neil found Mary Ann, her throat slit from ear to ear. It wasn't until after she'd been carted to a makeshift mortuary that jagged incisions were found in her abdomen.

Annie Chapman was born in Windsor in 1841. Shortly before her daughter's death in 1882, Annie abandoned her family and ended up in Whitechapel where she lived in a lodging house on Dorset Street. She led a rough life hawking her crochet work, selling flowers and other trifles, and occasionally resorting to prostitution to pay for a bed to sleep in each night. She was last seen at about 5.30 on the morning of 8 September 1888 talking to a man outside a house at 29 Hanbury Street. Just before 6 a.m., her body was found in the backyard of the property. No effort had been made to hide her body, and oddly enough, what most witnesses who saw her body remembered were her striped wool socks, which peeked from beneath her rumpled skirt. Her face and tongue were swollen, pointing to her being choked to death, and two incisions on her neck had nearly decapitated her. Her abdomen had been ravaged, intestines lifted from the abdominal cavity and placed on her shoulder, her female organs removed and missing.

Elizabeth Stride, a 45-year-old woman of Swedish descent ended up living from time to time at a common lodging house in Whitechapel. She was well known to the police having been arrested and convicted many times for drunkenness. She was last seen on 30 September 1888, at around 12.45 a.m. with a man outside Dutfields Yard on Berner Street. At 1 a.m. another man drove his horse and cart into the Yard, only to discover Elizabeth's still warm body. Elizabeth's throat had been slit. Her autopsy recorded bruises on her shoulders, supporting the belief that she had been pressed to the ground and held there while her throat was cut. Perhaps due to the arrival of the cart and horse into the Yard, no additional mutilations were found on Elizabeth's body. But the night was still young.

A short time later that night, Catherine Eddowes, a 46-year-old with three children, was out and about on the darkened streets. She and her common-law husband had separated due to heavy drinking and occasional bouts of violence that erupted between them. By 8.30 p.m. she had become so drunk that she was locked up by the police for her own welfare. They released her at about 1 a.m. and her mutilated body was discovered lying in the street in the early hours of 30 September 1888. Eddowes' throat had been cut to the bone bringing about immediate death after which she had been mutilated. Some internal organs had been removed. According to a witness, Eddowes apparently believed that she knew the identity of the Ripper and on the night of her death may have been in a hurry to meet someone.

Mary Jane Kelly, twenty-five, was the youngest of the Ripper victims, yet her life had been no easier than those lived by the others. She travelled with a man named Joseph Barnett but their existence was nomadic and they were continually moving due to drunkenness and rent owed. They eventually ended up at 13 Miller's Court on Dorset Street where Mary Jane was forced to resort to prostitution to pay her debts. On the evening of 8 November 1888 even though Mary Jane was in the first trimester of pregnancy and afraid of meeting the Ripper she took to the streets. Throughout the night, she was spotted by acquaintances on several occasions until around 2 a.m. when she was seen going into her room with a man. Mary Jane was found at 10.45 that morning, lying on the bed in her room. She had been mutilated beyond recognition; her heart had been excised and taken away.

Mary Ann 'Polly' Nicholls, 'Dark Annie' Chapman, Elizabeth 'Long Liz' Stride, Catherine Eddowes and

Mary Jane Kelly ... brutally murdered, mutilated and then forgotten, almost an afterthought to the memory of the madman who so brutally murdered them. Mary Ann and Annie Chapman were buried at Manor Park Cemetery, Elizabeth Stride in Pauper's Grave number 15509 in West Ham, Catherine Eddowes was laid to rest in an unmarked grave in Manor Park, while Mary Jane Kelly was buried at Walthamstow Roman Catholic Cemetery in Leytonstone.

Jack strikes again
Even as a child the tales of the Ripper and his crimes have so often figured in my life. Growing up I spent a lot of time with my aunt Grace and uncle Roy who lived in Leytonstone, east London. At the bottom of their road lay a vast cemetery and one day I remember wandering to those graves for no particular reason. As I walked through the graveyard I found myself inexplicably drawn towards a very simple, humble grave. There was no headstone to speak of but the flowers beside the grave, some fresh and some plastic, made me think that the grave must be for someone who had recently died. When I looked closely I saw that the grave belonged to Mary Kelly. Even though I was only eleven I recognised her name immediately as one of the Ripper's five victims. I sat down beside a collection of faded plastic roses and wept but didn't really know why.

As well as feeling intense empathy for the victims

for many years of my life I've also been haunted by the question marks Jack left behind. Just like many people I've felt the desire to discover who this man was and why he felt the compulsion to kill in the manner that he did. During one of my seminars in Eastbourne about two years ago the opportunity arose for me to investigate the case further when we put together a Jack the Ripper investigation for the hundred or so delegates present. Eight challenges were devised, relating to the Ripper case, each of which was hosted by one of the invited mediums working on the weekend. An assortment of psychic techniques were used such as tuning into photographs of the victims or Ripper suspects, and in the group assigned to me I decided to invite my students to step back in time with me to the night that the Ripper's third victim, Elizabeth Stride, was murdered.

When I'm attempting to step back in time in my mind I usually state out loud the year, the month, the day, the time, and the name of the person or situation I am trying to invoke. Then I go back in my mind to view and glean all I can from the images, smells and sounds that flood my mind. Most of the time when I do this I feel rooted to the spot, my head begins to spin and it's as if I'm actually stepping back in time. It's an intense and powerful experience and when performed as a guided visualisation with a group of people the results produced by the collective thought energy can produce spectacular results.

I prepared the room carefully before the group entered. I removed all furniture except for chairs for the group to sit on. Instead of light bulbs I used candles and I turned off the central heating and left all the windows slightly open so that a cool breeze filled the room. I wanted to create an atmosphere that would make it easier for them to imagine that they were really travelling back in time to the desolate streets of London's East End.

As the group settled down and took their seats around me, I told them to close their eyes and take a deep breath. 'It's dark and damp, we're outside, the date is thirtieth September eighteen eighty-eight and we're in the Dutfields Yard area of London,' I told them.

Encouraged by the obvious commitment of my group to this exercise I continued.

'I want you to imagine that Jack is walking towards us. He cannot see us but we can see him. Don't be afraid of him as fear will attract his attention and this is not what we want because if he knows we are watching he will try to mislead us and hamper our attempts to see who he is. We are silent witnesses not to the murders but to him. We aren't going to get sucked into the fear and the gore. We are going to sidestep the murders and follow him in our minds.'

My group visualised the things I was saying and to be honest for some it was only that – a visualisation – but for others, as I discovered at the end of the session when we had a group discussion, they saw what I saw.

We saw him walk towards us and then the vision took on a life of its own. We saw a cat pass him. We heard the sound of hushed conversations in the street and the sound of his smart heeled shoes on the pavement and breathed in the stench of rotten food, excrement and dirt from the streets. The next thing we were aware of was a carriage ride and a broken conversation between the Ripper and the driver. We noted the air of familiarity between them. We sat beside the Ripper in the carriage and for an instant it was as if he knew we were there with him but couldn't see us. We saw a man with a dark moustache. He was wearing dark trousers and a black coat; black so that the bloodstains were masked. He was a thickset man with a strong back as though he was able and used to lifting heavy weights. There was also a keen smell of camphor about him and the noted appearance of a scar running across his top and bottom lip. We saw his small but strong hands and the dark hair that covered them. His nails were chipped but well clipped. We heard the cries of Elizabeth. We felt his fury. We smelt the wet clothes and the blood and saw the cloths he used to clean his hands.

Then as if we were jumping forward in time we saw him alight from the carriage and walk towards a large door. I heard myself saying aloud to the group; 'What colour is the door?'

'It's black with brass handles,' they all said in unison.

The door opened and he stepped into a hall and as he did we all saw that the floor inside was black and white like a chessboard. There was a chandelier above us and in the distance rooms with men in them. It had the feel of a Masonic lodge or a gentleman's club and it was somewhere he was staying or at least was familiar with.

The door closed shut and we were left standing cold and alone on the street outside.

The visualisation ended and as I helped everyone adjust again to their normal surroundings it was clear that those within the group who had witnessed what I witnessed were visibly shaken by the experience. It was as if we had come face to face with the Ripper.

Ripperology

In recent years I have taken part in a television documentary about the Ripper murders, spoken to journalists, and walked the streets of Whitechapel with book researchers all wanting 'my take' on the events of 1888. This has allowed me to combine my psychic tools of investigation with the insights of some of the world experts in Ripperology. Each time I re-open this case, I hope it will yield important new leads or provide fresh insight. It would, of course, be easy for me to research on the internet and consult Ripper textbooks but of course this would defeat the purpose of the exercise. I need an open mind and from past experience I know having too much information and detail about a case has the opposite effect and clouds my vision.

Accepting an invitation from a leading Ripper expert, to accompany him on an investigation into the Ripper murders, I found myself again at the final resting place of Mary Kelly. As I stood once again before the grave I experienced the same overwhelming urge to cry as I had experienced all those years ago as a child. That day we visited many of the key sites, walking down the same streets that Jack himself would have walked many years before. We finally arrived at a large warehouse where Miller Court had once stood. I knew this spot was as close as we could get to the home of Mary Kelly and the place where she had lost her life. Embracing this knowledge I fixed my eyes on the building in front of me, willing myself to 'see' glimpses of the past that might help me in my quest to uncover the truth behind this baffling mystery. For some time nothing happened, I was beginning to think that this might be a waste of time when suddenly the warehouse began to disappear and in its place I saw rows of old houses divided by a labyrinth of alley-ways. Concentrating on the image in front of me, I became aware that day had turned to night and I was feeling a little afraid. I was startled at first, then gathering my thoughts I allowed myself to enter the alley-way ahead. It felt as though I was being pulled by an unseen force and eventually I found myself standing at the door of a rather dilapidated building. I instinctively knew this was the home of Mary Kelly, the door opened and I stepped in, I could see her bed and fireplace, and the fire embers were still warm. My heart began to beat hard in my chest, I could hear a lady's voice behind me, I turned quickly and there standing before me was Mary Kelly. She smiled and lifted her hand and reached out to touch my face, I was looking at her and she was looking at me. As though time stood still our eyes met and held each other's gaze for what felt like hours. I could feel her sadness and once more I started to cry. Then without warning I felt the presence of a man at my side and without hesitation he stepped in front of me. 'Oh my God, it's him,' I wanted to scream out loud, I wanted to run and get out of this place and to warn Mary that she was in mortal danger. Then I felt my legs give way and fell to the ground and I was back in the present day, shaking from head to foot, as I tried to regain my composure.

Standing there I began to speak and heard myself say, 'the Ripper killed twelve women'. I 'knew' that his targets were not prostitutes as such but women in general. I felt stained by his presence and asked the spirits to help me leave that place immediately.

From that day I felt I knew the Ripper, a part of him was familiar to me and I became determined to uncover his identity. I was, however, aware that the Ripper had been elusive in life and the chances were that he had held onto his mask of anonymity in the next life. Disappearing into the shadows after each of his grotesque crimes, nothing much seems to have changed since his own death. I even began to wonder if in death he had the ability to produce a smokescreen in my mind, to maintain his identity some one hundred and twenty years later. Or it could have been that the intense fascination of this case over many years with so many potential suspects and theories had created a haze of possibilities and I was finding it hard to see through all that.

The more I got involved in the case for the documentary the greater the confusion seemed. I really needed to find a way forward and the spirits finally gave me the clarity I had been searching for during a reading for Janice Wood, the great-great-great-granddaughter of the Ripper's fourth victim Catherine Eddowes.

My reading with Janice Wood

I was nervous and it wasn't easy for Janice to relax but eventually I was able to reassure her that we would take things slowly and gently and if at any point she felt uncomfortable we would stop. I told her that I knew very little about Catherine Eddowes apart from the most basic details and that all I had been given to work with was a photograph from Catherine's autopsy.

Concentrating on the photograph in my hand I closed my eyes and asked the spirits to bring forward information; after a while a very faint image of a lady in Victorian clothing came into mind. As it did my throat became dry and hoarse and I had to clear my throat several times before I could speak. Janice leaned forward as if to encourage me and her positive energy strengthened my link with Catherine. 'She's with me now,' I told Janice. 'As I merge with her energy I can tell she had had a terribly hard life.' I felt a little light-headed. 'I can see her walking at night with another woman. The other woman is clearly younger than her. I can see the two of them part company.' Then, as before, I felt the Ripper at my side and as though I was looking through his eyes, I saw what he saw, I also knew that he wanted the other woman, not Catherine at all.

I had to take a glass of water to continue as my throat was getting too dry and was so sore it was hard to speak. 'There was something wrong with her chest. She wasn't well. This is a silly detail but she had holes in her shoes. She's telling me she was at a desperate point in her life. She was a lot older than the other woman and I can sense clearly that she was not the intended victim. The other girl was but when she wandered away the Ripper was in such a frenzied state that anyone would do.'

Encouraged again by Janice's positive energy I continued. 'I think the Ripper was high when she was murdered. There was a chemical smell on his breath and this might explain why he took such chances. He was high and had lost his sense of caution as you do when you are drunk. Catherine tells me he was quite a small man really. She remembers dark eyes and a black moustache.'

Taking another sip of water I allowed my attention to focus even harder on Catherine and the image of two men suddenly flashed into my mind. 'I think there were two involved in the murder. One was on lookout and a helper. He had a carriage standing by. The name John or James comes forward clearly. I also think there were a lot more victims than the ones we know.'

I wanted to return my focus to Catherine as it kept slipping to the Ripper and his possible accomplice so I held her photograph close to my chest to tune in once again to her energy. Her image appeared clearly and sharply in my mind and then the messages came flooding in.

'There was some part of Catherine's body that couldn't be found. He took a memento from her body but this was after she died. I feel that she died very quickly. To be honest I don't think she understood what was going on. Something went over her face and then everything went black. I'm also getting the sense that in some ways she welcomed the release of death. Life had just got too hard, too hard for her. I'm approaching her murder with feelings of sorrow but she won't let me express them. I can't be tragic with Catherine. She is a beautiful spirit woman now who is free. She says she is happy to meet you Janice. She wants you to know that she has left all of it behind and she wants you and your family to leave all of it behind too. She is beautiful, really beautiful in spirit; almost like an angel.'

My link faded and then vanished and I reluctantly brought the reading to a close. The clarity with which Catherine had finally appeared and her radiance had taken even me by surprise.

As she was leaving Janice told me she had found the session very helpful and it was reassuring for her to know that Catherine's spirit looked so beautiful now. I was able to explain to Janice that it was significant that the Ripper's spirit had paled into insignificance and nothingness behind Catherine's clarity. This was because he would have gone to a lower, darker, less evolved realm when he passed over and would be there with other like-minded souls until the time came when he fully understood the implications of his actions. To do this he may have to reincarnate many times over and to choose lives of selfless devotion to others or he may have to experience the same pain, hurt, fear and horror he had caused others. Whatever his fate it would take a very long time for him to repay the karmic debt he had incurred for his vicious crimes.

The hunt continues

My reading with Janice had not produced as many significant new leads as I would perhaps have liked but it was important in another way. Focusing my energies on one of the victims rather than the Ripper himself had created feelings of resolution and completeness that I hadn't been able to experience before when dealing with the case.

Previously, whenever I was working on or thinking about the case I had mainly linked into the confusion, fear and pain surrounding the case and amid all that there was a restless desire to obliterate the uncertainty and find out who Jack was and why he killed. In some ways I may even have been tapping into Jack's compulsive nature but after the reading with Janice I felt calmer than before. I feel strongly that I will work on this case in the future and who knows what will come of that. Perhaps in the past I'd been focusing too much energy on Jack and this had created so many possibilities that I'd lost sight of the victims. I realised that my job as a medium regarding this case may not necessarily be to find out who Jack was but to turn the spotlight on the victims – to the beautiful spirits of Mary Ann Nicholls, Annie Chapman, Elizabeth Stride, Catherine Eddowes and Mary Kelly – and to cast Jack's spirit back into the darkness and the shadows where he belongs.

8

THE SECRET OF RENNES-LE-CHÂTEAU

Imagine arriving at an airport in France with no idea where you are going next. Imagine being greeted by a television crew who check you into a nearby hotel and that at the hotel comfort is clearly not a consideration and hospitality definitely off the menu. Imagine staying in a dingy room with ghastly 1970s furnishings on your own for a night and a day feeling tired and hungry but anxious about stepping outside to get some food and fresh air because you can't speak the language, haven't a clue where you are and the television crew are monitoring your every move. Imagine being bundled into a car on a boiling hot day and asked to wear a blindfold as the car drives for hours down bumpy and dusty road after bumpy and dusty road to a mystery location. With your blindfold still on imagine being dragged by the arm up some stairs and pushed through creaking doors. Imagine being asked to take the blindfold off and 'perform'.

There's no doubt my life as a television psychic medium (for want of a better description) has its upsides and I'm not complaining but there are times when I feel tired and jaded just like anyone else and my mystery trip to France for Discovery channel's *Legend Detectives* series was definitely one of those times. I was fed up, hungry and irritable and all the cloak and dagger stuff to ensure absolute secrecy for the programme certainly wasn't really the ideal way to help me create the right state of mind to link with spirit. But I'm not a quitter. I had come this far and I certainly wasn't going to give up now.

When I was asked to take the blindfold off I actually didn't want to. I was finding the blanket of darkness strangely comforting and wanted to ask the crew if I could keep it on for a while longer. I needed time to centre and calm myself. Not an easy task when the nervous coughs and impatient footsteps of the camera crew all around me were not only distracting but also putting me under incredible pressure to perform. (One thing I've learned over the years is that putting too much pressure on the spirit world and myself can often have the opposite effect!) I needed time to relax and to create an atmosphere of harmony within me. I took several deep breaths and as I did I slowly began to drink in the atmosphere around me. I had a gut feeling that I was standing inside a church. I also knew that I was standing in a place soaked in mystery and that the mystery was over one hundred years old and involved a priest.

Without warning and without my consent the blindfold was yanked off. I needed a few moments to regain my composure, and for my eyes to adjust to the light. As I stumbled slightly feeling my way I became aware of my surroundings and saw that I was indeed standing in a small church but it didn't look like an ordinary church; there were amazing carvings and coded symbols everywhere. During the time I spent within its walls I was bombarded with more information in such a short time, than I have ever received before. Breathing in the musky air that surrounded me visions and voices came thick and fast and the word 'treasure' shot into my mind, closely followed by the word 'secret', and then the vivid image of a priest digging inside the church, behind the altar and under the floor. I also saw an image in my mind of a skeleton, with blinding clarity the skeleton began to take the form of a woman and in that instant I was told by my spirit guide Star that the skeleton belonged to Mary Magdalene, followed by a feeling that she had lived and died in France. It was at this point that I thought I had entered the twilight zone! I was flooded with doubt and felt desperate for confirmation. Surely I had to be mistaken, but the images had been clear and strong I couldn't deny or explain them.

Reading all this in 2007/8 you might think that my insights were not a big deal but you need to understand that I took part in the documentary before Da Vinci Code mania had hit the bookshops and the media and certainly before I had heard anytime about it. For me it was only when Dan Brown's best-seller turned the spotlight on the bloodline of Jesus and Mary Magdalene that I realised my visions that day in the Church of Mary Magdalene had been more accurate than I had understood at the time. My visions had predicted something incredible. It had shown me that Mary had woken up from a long slumber; her story was ready to breathe again.

I looked around me hoping for some encouragement, but the camera crew were giving nothing away and I was handed a picture of a man who was clearly a priest. I knew instantly that he was a key to the puzzle of this church and that he was the keeper of a great secret. I also knew that he would die to protect his secret and that this secret was of great spiritual significance. In my mind I saw this man standing with four or five other priests studying an ancient text. They were a brotherhood of priests sworn to protect this secret.

Obviously excited by what I was sensing, the crew bundled me into the car again. I didn't feel nearly so fed up this time as the powerful image of Mary Magdalene had somehow aroused my curiosity and given me a huge energy boost. After driving for a while down more bumpy roads the car screeched to a halt and I was pulled out and taken again by the arm to another location, outdoors this time. When we reached the selected spot I found myself standing in front of a grave belonging to a man called Abbé Gélis who had died in 1897. As soon as I saw the grave everything flashed red before my eyes. My head throbbed unbearably as images of a man's skull being crushed and a body arranged on the floor as if in prayer darted through my mind. I told the crew I suspected that this man had been murdered by two men and another man was involved in some way and that he had been killed because he knew too much. I didn't think the man who murdered him was the priest whose photograph I had been shown earlier but I was convinced that this priest knew about the murder and was involved on some level.

After my experience in the church and now by the graveyard I wasn't feeling tired anymore; in fact, I had never felt fitter and more energetic. I knew I was on to something and unusually for me felt compelled to do some research of my own before the final day of filming. I normally never do this when I'm involved in a psychic investigation but I knew without a doubt that this investigation was unlike any other I had ever done. I also knew that the events I was trying to tap into were centuries old and to establish a psychic link so far in the past I really needed more facts to work with. I purchased some local guides to the area in English and found out that Rennes-le-Château was, as I suspected, a place steeped in mystery and legend. For those of you not entirely familiar with the story, or in a need of a recap, here's a brief summary.

THE SEARCH FOR HIDDEN TREASURE

The Rennes-le-Château myth starts in 1969, when Henry Lincoln read a thriller by French author Gérard de Sède, titled *Le tresor maudit* (The Cursed Treasure). In the fictional story, the treasure of the title had been found around 1891 by the priest of Rennes-le-Château after he deciphered some old documents hidden in the local church.

The priest was Bérenger Saunière, who had been the priest of Rennes-le-Château since 1885. Rennes-le-Château sits on top of a hill, about forty kilometres from Carcassonne, in the South of France.

The church, dedicated to Mary Magdalene, was almost in ruins when Saunière arrived. Having raised some money, the priest started restoration around 1887. During his work excavating and rebuilding the church, Saunière allegedly came across a number of coded parchments hidden within Visigothic pillars. Consulting with his close friend Abbé Henri Boudet, the priest of the neighbouring village of Rennes-les-Bains, Saunière then apparently left for Paris where he talked to specialists at the church of St Sulpice.

It is alleged that the author of the parchments was the Abbé Antoine Bigou, who may have written them – or at least secreted them – in 1781, more than a century before Saunière's time. Bigou was the confessor to Marie d'Hautpoul, a local noble woman.

The parchments were decoded to reveal the following cryptic messages:

This Treasure Belongs To Dagobert II King And To Sion And He Is There Dead
Shepherdess No Temptation That Poussin Teniers Hold The Key Peace 681 By The Cross And This Horse Of God I Complete This Daemon Guardian At Midday/Midnight Blue Apples

Meanwhile, work at the church continued, a stone slab was found under the floor, but only Saunière had access to it and could see what was behind it. From that moment on, the priest began long and secretive searches of the surrounding area, and after that, the restorations started once again. This time, however, funds seemed limitless, and Saunière – formerly an austere religious man who subsisted on a minuscule pay packet – used them to buy land and to build a number of constructions around his parish church, including a bizarre Tower of Magdala honouring Mary Magdalene. He also filled the church with mysterious statues and had various Latin inscriptions written all around the place.

Much has been made of Saunière's restoration of the Church of St Magdalene and the strange inscriptions. Above the entry lintel Saunière installed the Latin verse *Terribilis Est Locus Iste* – in English 'This is a Terrible Place'. Inside stands a statue of a demon, perhaps the guardian of treasure 'Asmodeus', beneath the water stoup. Opposite this demon, across a chess-board chequered floor is a statue of Jesus. The Stations of the Cross are said to have strange anomalies in their depictions, hinting at some heretical belief. And statues of Joseph and Mary, each holding a baby, stand either side of the altar. Some have surmised that these statues might be intended to represent Jesus and Mary Magdalene – a clue to a possible continuation of Jesus' bloodline.

All was fine for Saunière until the local Catholic Church hierarchy changed. A new regional bishop called Saunière to task for his obvious wealth, accusing him of simony – selling masses. Saunière ignored the requests for explanation, eventually quitting the priesthood rather than divulging his monetary source. On 17 January 1917, Saunière apparently had a stroke and died five days later. Local lore says that the priest who arrived to give last rites to Saunière denied him absolution based on his confession. It is also said that a strange memorial was held for the dead priest – his body was seated out on a balcony where mourners walked past plucking red pompoms from the shawl that covered him.

When relatives of Saunière enquired about his will, they were surprised to find that the priest had signed over all of his possessions – before his death – to his housekeeper Marie Denarnaud. The most probable explanation for this is that Marie was more than just

Saunière's housekeeper, she was his confidante or perhaps even his lover. Marie lived much longer than Saunière, dying in 1953. It is said that she told villagers that they 'walked on gold', and promised one day to reveal her secret to her caretaker during her later years, M. Nöel Corbu. Unfortunately, her affliction by a stroke shortly before her death left her unable to communicate, taking the secret to her grave.

This secret has variously been guessed as either a material treasure or some great secret of history – most notably that Jesus Christ sired children and his bloodline continued as a 'royal lineage'. With such notions in hand, Saunière could have turned Christianity on its head and inspired a whole new interpretation of world history. So why not use it to blackmail the Vatican and get rich by these means?

The story of Bérenger Saunière came to the attention of the French public around 1956, after Nöel Corbu told his story to reporters from a regional newspaper, *La Dépêche du Midi*. From this point onwards, Rennes-le-Château became known in French folklore as a 'treasure-town'. In 1962, an individual by the name of Gérard de Sède published his book *Le Trésor Maudit* (The Accursed Treasure), a key moment in the history of the mystery because, in 1969, a writer/producer for the BBC named Henry Lincoln happened across the book while on holiday in France, and after decoding some of Saunière's alleged parchments was hooked on finding a solution.

Lincoln pitched the storyline to the BBC for a documentary, and they agreed to let him pursue it. Lincoln's research began a second episode to the mystery of Rennes-le-Château – the unveiling of a secret society with reputedly ancient roots and modern power, the Prieure de Sion (Priory of Sion).

Lincoln went on to make three full-length documentaries on the subject of Rennes-le-Château and the Priory of Sion during the 1970s. When the subject became too far-ranging for him to handle on his own, he joined with two other researchers, Michael Baigent and Richard Leigh. This trio went on to publish the definitive popular work on the topic in 1982, *The Holy Blood and the Holy Grail,* a bestselling book in the millions, which still garners an audience (ever-growing after the publication of Dan Brown's referential novel, *The Da Vinci Code.*)

In the hands of Lincoln, Baigent and Leigh the mystery grew into a full-blown historical investigation which encompassed scepticism of the Gospel stories, occult secrets of the medieval Knights Templar and Cathars, and a great secret: that the bloodline of Jesus continued through Mary Magdalene and the Dark Ages French lineage of the Merovingians, and still persists due to the efforts of the Priory of Sion to protect it. A number of documents purportedly belonging to this organisation have been 'uncovered', which add to the mystery.

Like everyone else reading all this for the first time

my first reaction was, 'Wow! This is mind blowing stuff.' Part of me was drawn in by it all but another part was shocked and a little scared by the suggestion that the 'royal blood' is that of Jesus Christ, who had a child, Sarah, and the bloodline secretly survived and continued for 400 years, up to the Merovingian dynasty of the Franks of dark-age Europe. According to legend Jesus died an old man in France, where he fled with his family to escape prosecution, and was buried alongside Mary at Rennes-le-Château at a mystery location.

This incredible story was supposedly kept secret for two millennia by the Priory of Sion, a mysterious sect that is said to have also founded the Order of the Templars. Notwithstanding the secrecy, clues to this conceded story were scattered throughout the centuries by some initiates belonging to the Priory, such as Leonardo da Vinci, Isaac Newton, Victor Hugo, and Claude Debussy. This was how Lincoln and friends were allegedly able to reassemble the story, un-code hidden names, enigmas and wordplays, and find hints hidden in various paintings.

With so much controversial material to take in my head literally hurt thinking about it. But was it all true? Could it be true? My vision in the church had certainly given me reason to believe that it could well be true, but then I could also have been tapping into the many legends and stories that had been created here.

I needed to keep things real and so I decided to see what the sceptics had to say and as I did I realised that there were a number of alternative and perfectly plausible explanations for Saunière's riches. I had to consider them as well if I was to come to any kind of conclusion.

The plot thickens

I'd uncovered the story as told by Lincoln and his team but as I soon discovered the 'facts' were in many cases quite different, unproven or at least open to different interpretations. For example, the inscription that reads, 'This place is terrifying' actually is a biblical quotation (Genesis 28:17) meaning 'This place is wonderful'. Another inscription that appears at the base of a crucifix, *Christus A.O.M.P.S. Defendit*, has been translated by some as: *Christus Antiquus Ordo Mysticusque Prioratus Sionis Defendit* (Christ defends the ancient mystical order of the Priory of Sion). In reality, however, it is a common phrase used in some Catholic inscriptions, like the one in Rome on Pope Sisto V's obelisk: *Christus Ab Omni Malo Plebem Suam Defendat* (Christ defends his people against every evil).

As for the documents and the tombs of Magdalene and Christ neither of them have been discovered to offer conclusive proof. However, it appeared to be true that Saunière probably did find some valuable artifacts during restorations of the church. He noted such a discovery in his notebooks and tried to keep it secret in order to sell the objects and raise money. He also started to excavate the church's surroundings, hoping to find more.

Is this, then, the true and only source of Saunière's sudden wealth? Or could he have, as some believe, stumbled across buried treasure. It's possible, for example, that the treasure belonged to a mysterious Order of immensely rich warrior monks, the Knights Templar, who were active in the area.

Another explanation is that in its heyday, during the latter half of the first millennium, this tiny little village, known then as Rhaede, was the third largest city of the kingdom of the Visigoths. The Visigoths had in their possession the treasure from the Temple at Jerusalem and its legendary Great Table and Menorah, a huge seven-branched candlestick, both made of solid gold – both having disappeared in the area at the beginning of the sixth century AD.

Darker still, this land, part of a larger region known as the Languedoc, was the victim of one of the most shameful episodes in European history – Europe's first genocide when a Christian sect known as the Cathars was seen by the Church of Rome as a threat to its very existence so the Pope authorised a crusade of extermination against them. Before their final defeat they are said to have spirited away a treasure of immense spiritual importance, hidden at or near Rennes-le-Château and this treasure has never yet come to light.

It's also important to consider the integrity of Abbé Saunière himself. His life had a lot of rumours and question marks about it. Tales of visits to Paris, of friends in high places in celebrated and occult circles, of wining and dining famous people in his new villa, which he himself never lived in, of refusing to account for his expenditure and lifestyle to his bishop, only to the Vatican who passed no judgement on him, of his friendship with one priest who was rumoured to 'know secrets' and with another, Abbé Gèlis, who was the victim of a brutal murder. Some experts even suggest that his inexplicable wealth may simply have been the result of fraud.

When rumours spread around of Saunière's spending and extravagance, the local Catholic bishop investigated the matter, concluding that the priest had made his money from 'trafficking in Masses', a quite common wrongdoing among nineteenth- and early twentieth-century priests where they agreed for a fee to celebrate a great number of Masses for both the dead and the living.

Templars, Cathars, the Holy Grail, Mary Magdalene, the Tomb of Jesus, the Priory of Sion, the Devil's Treasure, Solomon's Treasure, the Ark of the Covenant, the Royal Line of Kings, the selling of illegal masses, raiding ancient burial sites, all these and more have been suggested as the secret of Rennes-le-Château but whatever it was that Abbé Saunière found or did, it kept him in comfort for most of his life.

With so many possibilities swimming around in my head I found it hard to sleep that night, eventually dozing off in the early hours. I awoke the next morning with a start and the sudden realisation that if I wanted to know the truth it would never be found in books. Lincoln's theory was compelling but for every theory or explanation put forward there was always going to be an equally compelling theory to answer it or contradict it. The only way for me to discover the secret of Rennes-le-Château was to leave the books and theories behind and ask the spirits to lead me to the treasure and to the truth.

Layers of history

I decided to spend the final day of my trip connecting with the atmosphere and energy of Rennes-le-Château. As I wandered around the village with the hot sun on my back, taking in the sights, smells and sounds of the breathtakingly beautiful surrounding countryside the line between past and present faded for me. I could hear the echoes from the past. I could hear the cries of children, the hushed conversation of lovers, the gossip of old men, the clash of swords, the neighing of horses and the sound of church bells ringing. Never before, or since, have I been to a place where I have been able to pick up so many layers of history and so many spirits. But this wasn't all. I was intensely aware that this was a holy and sacred place; a place of intrigue and death, yes, but also a place of pilgrimage and a secret that people would give their lives or even kill to protect.

Rennes-le-Château is a little village perched on a dusty hilltop in the French Pyrenees. Just looking round its tiny sun-baked cottages, its tumble-down medieval château, its ninth-century church restored in garish late nineteenth-century style, you would not think at first that this place might hold the keys to one of the world's great mysteries but as I wandered around the village that day I knew that it did. In my mind Mary Magdalene was without doubt there in spirit but she was much more than a myth or legend. I could see and feel her actually living and working there. She had been alive there. She had been a great teacher and healer in her day giving advice and spiritual nourishment to all who sought it.

As the layers of history faded in my mind and the veil between past and present returned I felt my legs go weak. I staggered to the side of the road and sat down with my head in my hands. I realised then that our world would never be the same again. But I didn't feel afraid, apprehensive or anxious about this change. Quite the opposite; I felt excited and incredibly blessed.

Not fallen, but free
The intense connection with spirit I sensed at Rennes-le-Château gave me the clarity I had been looking for, the certainty that no book or theory could ever give

me. I felt that Christ had lived and died there with Mary Magdalene I also knew that Mary would soon re-emerge into our consciousness. She would emerge for a reason. She had much to teach us. We needed her.

Like the story of Sleeping Beauty, Mary has been 'drugged' into unconsciousness for two thousand years, by an extraordinary effort to suppress 'the other half of the story' – her story. From the moment that Peter's Church formed the 'rock' and foundation of Christianity she was written out of accepted doctrine, save for references to her as a sinner, a fallen woman from whom seven devils were removed by Jesus, and the one who dried the sweat on his feet with her long hair.

Mary was suppressed because she was a dangerous figure to Christian 'authorities'. She represented a personal relationship with the divine without the need of priests and donations and bypassed the need for religion. She represented dangerous teachings such as the sacred marriage and sexuality as opposed to celibacy and virginity. Her existence proved sexuality was healthy rather than dysfunctional and 'dirty'. She celebrated the union of feminine with masculine not just in marriage but within every one of us.

Today, as I look back at the time I spent at Rennes-le-Château for the documentary my experiences and my feelings there make far better sense to me now than they did then. Through film, literature, revealed documents, and a growing interest in her story, it's clear that Magdalene is indeed finally rising from the hidden caves of our unconscious. The sacred feminine is re-emerging out of two thousand years of denial, banishment and a mistaken identity, to realise the fulfilment of a sacred trust, the blueprint for love and sacred union between opposites. But why, you may ask, did she wait so long? Why this sudden emergence of her story now?

I believe that Mary Magdalene is emerging now to show us a way forward at the beginning of the second millennium. It's a crucial turning point for us and for the earth we live on. She is calling on us to rewrite our global myth, and turn our attention away from the material towards the spiritual, towards love and respect for others. Her return signals a fusion of dimensions of consciousness that have been fragmented for two thousand years, giving birth now to a potent healing force that opens the Grail of the Heart.

While the 'Sacred Feminine' or 'Divine Feminine' means different things to each of us, for me at its most essential it is that life force within each man and woman to create, to nourish, to love and to be in cooperative relationship to others. In short, it is the spiritual force that unites rather than divides us. It is the loving force that elevates humanity and spirituality above sex, religion, race, culture or creed. Symbolised since before recorded time by female deities and earth goddesses and suppressed by the male-dominated, sky-god religions, leaving our world unbalanced and wracked with war, the Sacred Feminine is ready to show herself to all those willing to learn and grow. And in this materialistic age, with religious intolerance and the threat of global terrorism looming large, never have we needed her more!

Today, as more and more people discover the mystery of Rennes-le-Château, Mary Magdalene is no longer fallen, but free. Her freedom opens up the possibility for us all of a psychic revival, a return to spiritualism, a return to humanity. Forget conspiracy theories, hidden treasures, ancient tombs and secret societies. This spiritual revival is, I believe, the true mystery, the true revelation and the truly wonderful secret of Rennes-le-Château.

9

THE WITCHES OF CANEWDON

Growing up on Canvey Island I often heard stories about nearby Canewdon and its sinister reputation. In hushed tones I remember being told that Canewdon was a wicked and unlucky place. It was said to be haunted not just by witches and their familiars but also by a so-called grey lady who allegedly wafted around the medieval church of St Nicholas.

You can imagine how exciting all these eerie stories must have sounded to a young boy. They really fired my imagination and whenever Canewdon was mentioned in my mind's eye I'd see witches on broomsticks hurtling into the sky on moonlit nights, screeching and laughing and terrifying the people below and pale-faced lady ghosts moaning as they weaved their way among the graves. It wasn't until a few years later, however, when I was a young teenager that I was offered the chance to actually visit Canewdon and check it out for myself. One of my cousins had recently passed his driving test, and enjoying his newfound freedom, he offered to take me to Canewdon for Halloween.

At first, remembering the stories I'd heard since childhood, I felt a bit nervous about going but there was no way I was going to admit that I was scared to my 'grown up' cousin. Besides I was curious to see what all the fuss was about. So I got into my cousin's rusty Escort with music playing at full volume and we headed off; probably way over the speed limit. But my visit to Canewdon wasn't meant to be on this particular occasion. As we approached the village the local police were everywhere. They wouldn't let us in and it seemed that the whole of Canewdon had been cordoned off. At first we thought it might have been an accident or even a crime, only to discover that each year the village is a 'no go' area on the night of Halloween. It seems that the reputation of Canewdon's witches draws so many curious people and occultists to the village that the police frequently erect roadblocks preventing all but the villagers from entering. As we left I remember looking out of the back-seat window of our car at Canewdon's impressive but menacing church tower and thinking, 'there might be something in all of this after all'.

In the years that followed, even though Canewdon is close to where I live and the subject of the witches often arose in conversation with my friends, I never got a chance to really visit and explore the place for myself. So when I received a call in November 2006 from a local historian, called Jerry, who told me he was interested in the paranormal I listened with tremendous interest to what he had to say.

Jerry explained that until a few generations ago Canewdon was shunned by people in the surrounding district. It was considered an evil and unlucky place and visitors and travellers avoided it for fear of having their wagons bewitched. So great was the sinister reputation of the place that at one time all Canewdon people were thought to be witches and the village was called 'Witch Country'. It was also said that any woman seeking membership of the sinister sisterhood must dance round the church twelve times at midnight, whereupon the devil himself would appear to perform the necessary initiation. Even today, Jerry told me that Canewdon's sinister association was not quite dead and many locals still believe that six witches must always dwell in the village of Canewdon; if one dies another takes her place. As Jerry spoke I began to feel a bit apprehensive, perhaps my imagination was working overtime again just as it had done when I was a child, but I also didn't want to stop him talking. It was all so fascinating. Jerry went on to say that there was a reason why Canewdon was associated with witchcraft and devil worship. Salem, he explained, wasn't the only place to showcase hysteria against witches. Throughout England, there were numerous recorded witch trials and in those trials the village of Canewdon figured prominently. Many witches were tried and executed in Canewdon and hysterically accused of 'crimes' such as sending plagues of lice throughout the land, as well as other ghastly critters, to irritate their enemies.

This was a lot of information to take in and after giving me a few moments to reflect Jerry went on to ask if I would consider meeting him in Canewdon itself to see if I could pick anything up. He wanted to see whether the combined perspectives of a historian and a psychic could gather new evidence or bring new insights. Now don't ask me why, because I really don't know myself, but the very next evening I found myself in a pub called the Anchor, which is located in the heart of Canewdon village.

THE ANCHOR PUB

As I drove into Canewdon to meet Jerry I decided to have a look around the village first. I parked my car and walked down the high street dominated to the west by the imposing Church tower. The village seemed tiny; somehow in my mind it had appeared larger but there was plenty to catch my eye, including the village cage and the pond where witches were no doubt ducked in the old days. As I wandered around I didn't pick up any negative energies but I sensed how isolated the place must have felt to the clannish locals who lived there hundreds of years ago surrounded as it was by nothing but marshlands.

It was getting cold outside so I made my way to the Anchor pub. As I stepped inside a number of locals glanced at me and then immediately looked away. Although I certainly wasn't welcomed with open arms the place had a certain charm about it and I didn't want to leave. I walked to the bar and ordered an orange juice from the barmaid. She nodded and then gave me a very strange look that screamed 'you're not from these parts are you'. It was a bit unsettling but then I realised she wasn't looking at me at all she was actually looking over my head at someone who had just walked in and this person was heading straight towards me. It was Jerry, the historian.

Jerry ordered a drink and the two of us sat down to chat. I asked how I could help him and he explained that for years he had been fascinated by the history of Canewdon and the stories his grandmother had told him 'about the strange goings on'. He wanted my thoughts on the subject as a psychic and medium. We sat for quite a while talking about the work of a psychic medium and what it can bring to an investigation or a case study.

I explained to Jerry that in some instances psychics and mediums could yield information that cannot be obtained through conventional research or detective work. I told him that we have a wide assortment of tools we use which can help us see beyond the realms of known science and these include: dreams, which can sometimes provide valuable insights; dowsing, the ability to locate objects psychically by means of a pendulum or a pair of handheld rods; and psychometry, when an object worn or used by someone creates an emotional link and sends revealing images or feelings into the psychic's mind. I told him that I use all three of these techniques in my work but the one I rely on most is clairvoyance or my ability to see or sense what is not ordinarily detectable. This includes objects and events distantly located in time or space, apparitions and presences; in short an awareness of things without sensory means. I also told him I have the ability to hear voices without recourse to my brain's audio sensors and this is called clairaudience. Many mediums and psychics, like me, are not just clairvoyant and clairaudient but also clairsentient. Clairsentience, I continued, is the ability to receive information so overwhelmingly inclusive that it feels like a multi-dimensional knowingness. The energies I sense can be light or heavy, smooth or abrasive, prickly or gentle, peaceful and airy, or positive or negative. For example, when sensing a negative situation I can feel sick, while a positive experience may feel like butterflies in the stomach, or a sense of feeling safe, peaceful and light. In short, clairsentience is my gut feeling about something, someone or somewhere.

Encouraged by Jerry's obvious interest in the work I do, I told him that my psychic abilities also helped me to see moments or memories from the past. Tardis-like, my mind can travel in space and time and

I can step into a scene or situation from the past and by so doing can sometimes provide insights or add vital information to a case that cannot be unearthed by any other means. This really got Jerry excited and he begged me to see what I could pick up 'right now' in the pub. The pub wasn't very busy and so breaking my own rules of prying psychically for the sake of it, I tuned in. I closed my eyes and the instant I did I was racing back in time.

Seeing red

I heard whispers, screams and footsteps. Time vanished and I began to lose myself in the past. I wasn't sitting with Jerry anymore enjoying a chat and a drink, I was standing in a room upstairs in the pub. I felt as though I was being pushed with great force and now I was lying on a wooden floor. Splinters cut into my hands as I tried to get up. I couldn't breathe. I wasn't just scared. I was terrified. For a split second I wasn't myself anymore. I was a young woman wearing clothes that dated back two or three hundred years. I felt her fear but the fear wasn't for herself it was for her baby who was crying, screaming in the next room. Then I smelt alcohol. I knew that I was being beaten by a man, a brutish man with long red hair and tiny bloodshot eyes. As I turned around to look at him, I was able to see through her eyes and as I did, my heart skipped a beat. The man abusing her was filled with anger and hatred. He had a heavy jug in his hand and was lifting it above his head. I felt her anguish and then her blood on my face. Swallowing hard and overcome with emotion I forced myself to become a witness not a participant to the scene. I then saw the woman begging and pleading but the man lifted another jug and then another. The beating became more ferocious the more she begged for mercy.

I desperately wanted to help her but reminded myself that this was only the memory of an event not the actual event itself. The woman had long since passed into spirit and her pain had vanished into history. I was simply looking back in time and catching a glimpse of an event so powerful and painful that it had left a stain within the atmosphere of the pub, forever to exist, tangible only to those with a developed ability to see the past. In fact, some paranormal experts believe that many hauntings or sightings of ghosts can be explained in this way. There's even a technical name for it and that's residual haunting. A residual haunting is a playback of a past event. When a traumatic event or a time of heightened emotions occurs, the energy created is so strong that it gets trapped and repeats itself to those sensitive enough to pick up on it like a recording on an 'endless loop' of magnetic tape.

Jerry asked me if I was okay as by now I was hunched over the table with my head in my hands. I explained to him the things I had seen, and asked if there had been sightings of the ghost of a young woman in the pub itself. Jerry jumped up with excitement and said that his grandmother once told him the story of a young woman called Sarah who had connections with the Anchor pub. Back in the 1500s she had an affair with a wealthy landowner and became pregnant. The man's wife found out and told him to lock Sarah away. She was held in the building that later became the Anchor pub. After having the baby, Sarah was brutally murdered. Jerry also told me that many locals thought the pub was haunted by Sarah and that the landlady was so scared she often refused to lock up the pub on her own.

We both agreed that what I had seen in my vision could have been Sarah's death but it was too early to draw any firm conclusions. Either way Jerry seemed more than happy to accept it as a great possibility. Last orders were being called so I said goodbye to Jerry and wished him luck with his investigation. He told me that he had enjoyed the evening immensely and it had given him fresh insights that he could use. As we parted, without thinking how or why, I heard myself saying that I would definitely return to Canewdon sometime soon to continue the investigation.

I want to see more!
Witches or not, Canewdon had cast a spell over me. As I drove back home I couldn't stop thinking about the young woman and I wondered what had happened

to her child. That night I tried to sleep but couldn't. I tried everything to relax and unwind but nothing seemed to work; I did some ironing, read an extremely boring book, counted sheep, had several glasses of milk but at 2 a.m. I was still wide awake. I got out of bed and looked out of the window. The moon was almost full and the night was cold and sharp as the sky was clear and sparkling. I glanced up to see the stars and wondered what on earth I was doing getting so involved in this investigation into a world of super-stition, folklore and witchcraft. I must have stayed at the window staring at the night sky for more than twenty minutes or so. Then, just as my eyelids were finally getting heavy and bed became a comforting thought, I saw a shooting star. The star reminded me that there is so much more to heaven and earth than we realise and maybe I was drawn to this little village and couldn't stop thinking about it because Canewdon's past needed to be seen.

Wide awake and bursting with excitement I decided there and then to explore the case further not as I usually do – to help someone or to uncover something a previous investigation had missed – but for myself! I wanted to see how far I could look back and to test my own ability to see more of the story. Again I'm not sure why but I needed to see what I could pick up. I could, of course, have gone on the internet or grabbed some books about the history of Essex and

Canewdon but I can assure you that this is not the way I work and the things I'm writing here about my personal investigation of Canewdon are my own thoughts, my own visions and my own feelings about this most bewitching place.

The next day after a busy morning of readings I packed a small bag with a torch, a pen, a notebook and an extra jumper because it was freezing. I also decided to take a small tape recorder as I wanted to try some EVP (electronic voice phenomena). The basic idea behind EVP is the belief that spirits may find it possible to create a voice that is inaudible to the human ear but can be picked up by recording devices, such as tape recorders. If anything were picked up it wouldn't necessarily be heard at the time by me or anyone else present but might possibly be heard on playback. I've never worked directly with EVP before in my psychic investigations and this was my chance to experiment.

I arrived at Canewdon at around 4 p.m. and made some phone calls, mainly to tell people that I was going to be busy for the next few hours and not to call. Everyone I called wanted to know what I was up to but – and again this is unlike me – I didn't tell them that I was on my own and didn't really know why I was here at all! Then I turned my phone off, checked I had also packed a bottle of water and more importantly a couple of bars of chocolate and put a woolly hat on that my mum had bought me a few years ago, realising as I put it on that it was the first time I'd actually worn it. I then started walking down a small one-track road that led to St. Nicholas Church.

ST NICHOLAS CHURCH

St Nicholas Church was built by Henry V to celebrate his victory at Agincourt and as I headed towards it I admired the way it rose majestically above the bleak' expanse of wide-open countryside. I entered the churchyard itself and noticed its scattered, leaning gravestones and dense vegetation. The atmosphere was strangely subdued and gentle. It was hard to believe that the place had such a sinister reputation. But I knew that the belief that this church had a resident ghost was so strong that every Halloween the police still had to cordon off surrounding roads to prevent the hordes of ghost hunters who tried to make pilgrimages here.

Suddenly the wind picked up and I nearly lost my woolly hat. It started to drizzle too and for a moment I thought about turning back. What on earth was I doing here when I could be sitting at home in the warm with a cup of tea? But something made me walk towards to the church and as I did I couldn't help but look up at the church roof. There meeting my gaze and perched on the spire was the biggest, blackest and most dangerous looking raven I've even seen. Then almost on cue as if I was in a gothic novel or movie it cried out loudly as I passed by.

Rubbing my hands together to keep them warm I approached the church porch and hurried inside. I tried the solid wood door and to my grateful surprise it was open. I stepped inside quietly not sure if I'd be interrupting choir practice or maybe a church meeting, or even someone deep in prayer. Luckily the place was deserted. I've always loved visiting old churches and have the utmost respect for them so I spent a while looking around the place, admiring the stained glass windows and high ceilings, wondering as I always did how many years of sweat, tears, devotion and faith it took to build it. I ran my fingers over the carved oak pulpit and imagined what it would be like to talk to a congregation from its lofty heights. After turning the pages of the enormous and well-used bible I looked around for somewhere to sit. I sat on one of the pews at the back and quickly took off my woolly hat, reproaching myself for not doing this earlier out of respect. Then I closed my eyes and said the following words out loud: 'Allow me to see all that I can. Allow me to know all that I'm able. Allow me to feel all that is true.' I then focused all of my attention on my breathing and waited for the journey to begin.

Driven out

I don't know how long I sat waiting but it must have been for at least fifteen minutes. At first nothing happened but then a powerful and intense vision swept over and through me. I found myself hurtling back in time but this time I was surrounded by a group of people all pointing and shouting at me. I was being called a witch. I looked down at my legs. They were sore and bleeding and they had been tied together as were my hands. I expected to see a woman but the memories I was feeling and seeing were those of an old man and I knew his name was John.

It was important to distance myself from the memories so that I could view what was going on. My woolly hat was still in my hands and I clutched it tightly to remind myself that I was a silent witness not a participant. Feeling more grounded to the present and distanced from the past I saw that the old man was crying. He wasn't screaming out or protesting he was just crying. His hair and face was covered in dirt and he didn't have any clothes on. His tormentors, both men and women, were searching his body for markings. I heard one of them say in a voice hoarse from screaming, 'he'll have the mark on him all right'.

Then as though I had lost my place in a book and had been given a new chapter to read, I felt myself skip forward in time. This time I saw John being driven by horse and wagon out of the village. As the wagon raced away John's eyes met mine and there was a flicker of recognition between us. John could see me. I opened my eyes and thought I was starting to return to every day consciousness but then I hurtled backwards in time again. This time I found myself standing in the aisle of the church. I was an invisible witness to a busy Sunday service. It was clear to me from the way people were dressed that I was near to or close to the same time that I had received the vision of John. No exact dates flashed before me but I knew the world I was viewing was hundreds of years old.

As I wandered about the church and watched the congregation mouth the words of a prayer, their heads bowed, I noticed that a number of the women were wearing the same colour; a rather unusual mustard yellow. One wore a yellow pair of gloves, another wore a yellow bonnet, another wore a yellow ribbon in her hair and another had a yellow bag at her feet. I felt myself floating up to the chapel ceiling and as I looked down on the congregation below the colour yellow shone around these four women. I knew then that the yellow colour was something I was meant to notice as I might easily have missed it if I hadn't elevated. Until now I had witnessed the scene in silence; it was like watching a mute television screen but as soon as I noticed the yellow light coming from the women the voice of the vicar boomed out; he was delivering his sermon in a monotone voice. As he read from the Bible I saw that in his left hand he held a bookmark and the bookmark was also mustard yellow. It was then that I realised I had been spotted because all four women and the vicar looked in my direction at the same time. I don't think they saw me, but I knew they were aware of my presence and I knew that these four women, the vicar and John from my previous vision were all connected in some way. The lady with the yellow gloves smiled at me and the lady with the yellow bag nodded her head. After that flicker of recognition, just like the one John had given me in my previous vision, I jolted forward in time again and found myself back in the present day, sitting in the church.

It took a while to collect my thoughts and my mind was racing. Who were these people and what was the significance of the colour yellow? I asked the question and at the same time I already knew the answer. This may sound strange but when I see a vision I often get so much more than visual impressions; I know and taste and feel so much more, more than I realise at the time. So, although I was turning questions over in mind the answers were already there. I just needed a few moments to sort through the images and sensations swirling through my mind to find the answer.

In a flash of intuition I understood why I had felt a sense of peace and not fear when I entered the church. The people I had seen in my vision were witches or pagans who met under the cover of darkness to practise the arts of healing and prophecy. Many of these witches had psychic or mediumistic powers much like my own and they had seen me in the church watching them and John had seen me as he was being cast out of the village. They were a band of people who embraced nature and celebrated their belief in secret for fear of being driven out or persecuted. On the surface of things these people lived very ordinary Christian lives but they met at certain times of the month dictated by the waxing and waning of the moon, to evoke ancient healing powers. I sensed that Canewdon had a long heritage of drawing people, like them in the past and me in the present, with psychic or mediumistic powers to it, many of them not really knowing why but coming because the village had called them.

As a spiritual person I feel an affinity for witchcraft even though I am not a witch myself. Witchcraft is a belief system that worships the divine feminine principle and uses the powers of nature and the mind to bring about a desired effect. Witches are believed to possess psychic powers, like clairvoyance, and there was no doubt in my mind that in my visions six witches from Canewdon's past had seen me clairvoyantly. I was also convinced that these people were not evil and the 'magic' they practised was white. I knew that because the aura or energy vibration surrounding them all was the colour yellow and this colour represents wisdom, generosity of spirit and great spiritual development.

As I left the church I felt incredibly blessed to be born at a time when I could express and practise my beliefs and do my work openly without fear of persecution. It wasn't until 1951 that witchcraft ceased to be a crime in England, which really isn't that long ago if you think about it. I sincerely hoped that the band of people who 'saw' me had been comforted by their sense of me and the more tolerant and accepting future I had offered them a glimpse of.

Echoes from the past

Feeling energetic and uplifted I walked out of the church but I still couldn't bring myself to leave. The light was fading fast so I decided to take one last walk around the church grounds, within God's Acre. I switched on my torch as it was getting hard to see and wandered among the gravestones that jutted out of the earth like uneven teeth. Even though I was in a graveyard in an allegedly haunted location and the light was disappearing I wasn't scared at all. My visions in the church had taken away all fear and I knew that nothing would harm me here; I was among friends.

My stomach growled and I reached for a bar of chocolate in my bag. I had to take my Dictaphone out of the bag to reach my chocolate and this reminded me that I had wanted to try some EVP (Electronic Voice Phenomena) on this investigation. I inserted a blank tape and pressed both play and record and as I did I invited the spirits to leave their voices on the tape if they so wished. As the tape turned I silently walked to the church's west gate and stood listening, waiting and watching for what must have been quite a long time because when I finally looked up at the sky the stars were out and the moon was high. I shuddered with cold and I never thought I'd say this, but I was glad that my woolly hat was covering my ears; they would have been freezing by now without it. Taking a final look around to drink in the atmosphere one more time I decided it was time to call it a day, but just as I was about to switch my tape off I felt something gently brush my shoulder. I turned around expecting to see someone or something behind me but there was nobody, nothing there. Feeling a little unnerved I turned the tape off and headed towards the car. It was really cold by now and I ran as fast as my legs would carry me back to my car.

Two days later I remembered the tape and decided to play it to see if anything had been picked up. I pressed play and for a long time heard only the sound of me walking, coughing and occasionally yawning. Then out of the silence I heard as clear as day, three words, 'We're still here', followed by the sound of me turning around as an invisible hand touched me. The witches of Canewdon were reminding me not to forget them and in my heart I promised them that I never would and that's why this chapter is dedicated to them.

CLOSING THE CASE FILES

I'd like to take this opportunity to thank you for coming on this journey with me. It's been a wonderful privilege to re-open some of my case files, past and present, and share them with you. I hope they will help open your eyes to the wonderful possibilities that are out there for you, both in this life and the next.

In the next section of the book, 'Moving Through Grief', I suggest ways to come to terms with the devastating impact of the loss of a loved one from a spiritualist point of view. I also discuss when and how to contact a medium and, for those who prefer to work alone, how to listen to and let spirit in to your life.

AFTERWORD:
Moving Through Grief

When someone you love dies you can't physically hug, cry or laugh with them anymore but you can learn to experience them in a different way. They can stay alive in your heart and in your mind and in the belief that in spirit form they can be with you more intensely than ever before.

I've worked with hundreds of grieving relatives or partners over the years and I know, perhaps more than most, how heart-wrenching and painful death can be. And if the death is sudden or unexpected, or because of suicide or murder, those left behind face even more difficult challenges. Overwhelming emotions can leave you reeling. It may seem like your support system has vanished. And you may be consumed by feelings of anger and revenge or guilt, wondering if there's something you could have done or said to prevent your loved one's death or to clear the air if words were left unsaid.

In order to move beyond the pain of loss and grief

there are steps you can take to begin the process of healing and in most cases I would not necessarily recommend visiting a medium until these steps have been taken. The first is to experience your grief. In whatever way a loved one passes the pain created by loss is an emotional wound that needs healing. For healing to occur, you need to mourn the loss and all it represents. If you do not allow yourself to grieve, the wound may cover over but not heal completely and prevent you moving forward and fully experiencing your life.

WHAT TO EXPECT

Learning about grief is helpful. Although knowing what's normal does not erase the pain, it can reduce the fear. Although everyone experiences loss and grief, no two people respond to the same situation in exactly the same way.

The most common initial reaction to a significant loss is denial and shock. You may have felt, 'This can't really be happening', or 'It's a bad dream'. You may have felt emotionally numb. This numbness is said to be nature's way of helping us through an experience that otherwise would be overwhelmingly intolerable and painful. It serves to deaden the pain and give us the time we need to absorb what has happened, mobilise our internal resources, and prepare for the difficult times ahead.

Once the numbness lifts, you may be hit with the

reality of the loss. You are likely to experience a range of emotions from tremendous sadness to helplessness, anger, guilt, or fear. You may experience erratic shifts in mood.

Anger and guilt tend to be difficult emotions for many people. Guilty feelings may emerge from unreasonably believing that you could have prevented the loss, or that you somehow contributed to the loss. Anger is especially confusing when it is felt towards the person who died; yet, this feeling is common. It's important to remember that feelings are neither right or wrong, nor good or bad; they just are. Remember, it's what you do with your feelings that make them right or wrong. If you don't resolve these feelings, you may direct the anger at others in hurtful ways or become severely depressed.

Other reactions include feeling sad, depressed, unresolved, desperate, panicked, anxious, or overwhelmed. Additionally, the stress endured during grief may produce physical symptoms such as nausea, headaches, sore muscles, fatigue, insomnia, and loss of appetite. (If you are experiencing these, or other physical symptoms, be sure to see a physician for a more thorough evaluation.)

Again, people vary widely with respect to the degree that they grieve. Some people feel the impact of a loss immediately, while others may not feel the impact until months or years afterwards. Some people move through the grieving process fairly quickly, while others may grieve on and off for months, or even years. However, when people are able to move through the various phases of grief (disbelief, shock, anger, sadness), and experience and integrate the array of feelings tied to the loss, they are often able to finally accept the loss, and move on to new phases of their lives.

MOVING THROUGH GRIEF

Moving through grief requires taking one moment, one hour and one day at a time. At times, you may find it hard to believe you will ever get over the intense and painful feelings, but you will adjust if you give yourself time to heal.

To successfully move through your grief, you must experience the emotional pain. You can't deaden it, run away from it, or escape it in any other way if you are truly going to come out of it a whole and healthy person. While you will need support from others, there are things you can do to help yourself move through a loss experience and begin to put your life together again. Although I am not a trained counsellor or an expert in grief counselling, my advice comes from years of experience working with the bereaved.

First of all, accept and talk about your feelings
One of the most harmful things you can do is to bottle up your feelings. Denying or repressing feelings often intensifies and prolongs working through grief. Its

been said that sorrow which is never spoken is the heaviest load to bear. An old Turkish proverb states; 'He that conceals his grief finds no remedy for it.' People who avoid conscious grieving generally break down emotionally, physically, or both.

It's okay to cry. It's okay to be angry. It's okay to be sad. You may think you are going crazy. This is a common reaction. You are not losing your mind – you are only reacting to your loss.

Most people find that talking about their feelings helps them to deal with and accept their loss. Some find that doing something physical – for example, pounding a pillow or screaming out loud in a private place – is helpful. In whatever way you express your feelings, be sure it is not harmful to others or yourself.

If you don't let your feelings out, they will come out at some other time or in some other way. You may become depressed or physically ill. An emotion that is denied expression is not destroyed.

Expressing feelings and thoughts in a journal may be helpful. Write about your feelings.

I feel betrayed because . . .
I feel scared because . . .
I feel angry because . . .

Keeping a journal also can provide a way to measure your progress. It can help to look at what you wrote two or six months ago and compare it with the present.

Second, give yourself the time you need

Grieving takes time. It can't be hurried. Just as it takes time for broken bones to heal, it takes time for broken hearts and spirits to heal.

There is no fixed time period for grieving. It varies from person to person. However, many people do not understand grief and may think you can just 'snap out of it' or 'should be getting over it' much sooner than is realistic. Try not to judge yourself by the expectations of others.

Grieving is not something we can just 'snap out of'. One must grow out of it, and that takes time and effort.

Third, accept support from others

With a physical wound we allow others to take care of us, we also need to do the same with emotional wounds. Accept the support and help of others. Don't expect family and friends to 'read your mind' and know when you need help and the specific help you need – they can't. It's important, too, not to build a wall around yourself and distance yourself from others for fear of being hurt again.

If others do not offer help, ask for it. Often people don't help because they don't know what to do. They may be afraid of making a mistake – of saying or doing the 'wrong thing' – or feel awkward.

Find someone who will listen non-judgmentally and accept your feelings, and with whom you feel comfortable talking freely. Recognise that some of your family and friends may be uncomfortable with your feelings and want you to be your 'old self' again.

It's also often difficult for family to support each other when each family member is grieving. Communicating with family and respecting each family member's way of grieving are important to coping and growing as a family through grief.

If you don't have family or a friend you can talk to about your feelings, consider a support group. Attending a support group of persons experiencing a similar loss can be therapeutic and a source of hope, understanding and encouragement. Information about support groups in your area may be available from the pastoral care or social work department at the hospital, the local mental health centre, your clergy, hospice programme, or senior centre.

Fourth, resume your daily routine
Allow yourself time to recover from the initial shock but in most cases the sooner you can return to your daily activities, the better. Search for activities that are meaningful to you – this can help give a new purpose to life. Social activity in general has a positive influence on adjustment. Some people have found that one of the best ways to move through grief is to do something for someone else. This does not mean you forget what has happened but involvement in activities can help fill the void created by a loss.

For instance, making yourself get up at a certain time every day, writing a list of tasks for yourself and staying productive can give you a sense of control. If you once depended upon your partner to structure your life for you, you may find it particularly difficult to develop interests. That's why it's all the more important now to develop interests of your own.

Fifth, be good to yourself
The stress of grief can cause physical problems. Research shows that people who experience a significant loss, particularly the death of a loved one, are more likely to become ill within six months after the loss. This is also a time when you may be more accident prone and more vulnerable to a flare-up of an existing medical condition. Eating well, getting adequate sleep and rest, and exercising regularly are important. Exercise helps reduce stress, work off frustrations and aid sleep.

If you are under a doctor's care for a pre-existing medical condition, do not discontinue that care.

Avoid alcohol and unnecessary medications. A mild sedative or tranquilizer may provide some initial needed relief. However, drugs or alcohol taken to reduce or mask the pain are harmful – they only stop, delay, or prolong grief, which means you'll simply have to face the loss later. Sedating medication, if used at all, should only be a temporary measure to help you through the initial shock.

Being good to yourself also means going easy on

yourself. Postpone making major decisions – for example, moving, giving away possessions, or rein-vesting finances – until after the period of intense grief, if at all possible. Whatever can wait should wait.

Emotions impair judgment and major decisions made during a time of emotional upheaval are frequently regretted later. You need time to re-establish balance in your life, regain self-confidence, and find out what the 'new you' will need and want. Remaining in a familiar environment can provide a sense of security and stability at a time of emotional upheaval.

Finally, expect and prepare ahead for hard times
Evenings, weekends, or special events – birthdays, anniversaries, and holidays – are generally difficult during the first year following the death of a loved one. Analyse what it is that makes certain times especially difficult and then make specific plans for those times; schedule activities that you find particularly comforting during these time periods.

A certain day of the week or time of day, favourite foods, colognes, music, or events can also make you painfully aware of a person's absence. Any place or event that is closely associated with a person who died – going to church or participating in certain activities – may be extremely painful for you.

Holidays, and especially family gatherings, can be particularly difficult after a death. These events may only serve to remind you of the changes in your life.

Festive occasions, especially shortly after a death, are often difficult because of the expectation that we 'should' be happy, 'should' be having a great time. The difference between these 'shoulds' and our actual feelings often increase our sense of loss. To make these events easier:

- Plan how you will spend the special days.
- Ask yourself what traditions you want to keep – what really has to be done versus what you feel you 'ought to do'.
- Share your feelings with family.
- Talk honestly with family members as you make your plans.
- Seek professional help if needed.

If you experience a sense of guilt or worthlessness because you are alive and your loved one is not, try not to indulge in it. You are unique. There is no one on earth like you and your energy is needed here. You have a purpose and a destiny to fulfil and other people need your light. If you feel all alone perhaps one day you will be able to help someone else going through the same pain.

If your grief persists, if you lash out in anger at people around you, if you become depressed and feel life is hopeless, or if you are considering suicide, seek professional help. Psychologists, psychiatrists, clergy, social workers, counsellors and grief therapists can all help a person who is grieving. They can help us adjust to loss, find solutions to difficult situations and resolve feelings such as anger, guilt, or despair, which may keep us from fully functioning.

MOVING ON

There are no easy answers or short cuts to moving through grief. It's a difficult process and it takes time – sometimes a very long time. It cannot be accomplished without pain, but believe me the pain will diminish. Remember, too, it is not possible to get back to 'normal', if 'normal' means the way things used to be. Life is about change and your life has changed.

Most importantly, have realistic expectations of yourself. Moving on from grief takes time and hard work. You will get better. Although some days you may just seem to exist, gradually you will feel better and better. Grief is like an ocean – it ebbs and flows; sometimes it rolls in gently; other times it pounds hard. With time, the pain of grief will lessen and you will come to a place where 'memories are sweet, not painful as they were at first'.

Though loss is painful, it is a part of life and every one of us will experience it at some time or other. Grieving is universal but it is also personal and there is no way of judging the amount of time any person will need to heal and move on with their life. So take your time and heal in your own way. When the going gets tough, which it will from time to time, you will always have special memories to grab hold of and you will always have your loved one around you even if you aren't aware of it.

Successful adjustment does not mean you become 'your old self again'. You will be changed by the experience – life will be forever different. However, you do have a choice. You can choose to celebrate and treasure the memories of your loved one or become embittered and it's obvious which path the spirit of a lost loved one would prefer you to take. Successful adjustment does not mean you forget the person who died or whatever loss you have experienced. It means that you are able to remember and talk about 'what was' without it causing the 'stabbing pain' it once did.

Whenever you love someone you give away a part of yourself and that is a beautiful thing as long as you don't compromise yourself too much. If too much of your identity was tied to someone else their loss can lead to a sense of emptiness but it doesn't have to be that way. When a loved one dies amid all that pain you also have the opportunity to reclaim a part of yourself you gave away; the creative power that is yours. Obviously this isn't something that is going to happen overnight but if you allow yourself to experience your grief fully and give yourself time to acknowledge your loss, eventually your strength and potential will return to you. You will rediscover who you truly are and there can be nothing more reassuring and beautiful than that.

MAKING CONTACT

How often after a loss should you wait to make contact?

I'm often asked this question and my answer is always the same. Spirits are able to communicate immediately after passing over. There is no time of adjustment needed for them to reach out, and very often they are as eager to reach out to us in those first critical hours as we are to hear from them. The issue, however, is not with the spirits but rather with us.

The right time to make communication with a departed loved one is after some time and perspective. I get many desperate calls from people who feel they must make communication right away, but I stress that there needs to be a period of acceptance and understanding of the passing first. There are many wonderful things that happen as a result of making contact with a departed loved one in spirit, but this contact cannot bring a loved one back or keep them on the earth. Once acceptance of the physical loss has taken place and you feel strong enough emotionally, you can begin the process of attempting to make contact with a departed loved one, either through a medium or, if you possess a strong psychic or mediumistic link, on your own.

Spirits are with us all the time and keen to make contact and let us know they are around but in order for a connection to be established you need to approach things in the right frame of mind. First of all you need discipline and a serious state of mind; spirits won't just magically appear if you light a candle and want to have some fun with your friends. The spirits will not respond to curiosity or a sense of mischief but they can respond to an open mind and a sense of respect, humility, love, discipline and reverence.

Before attempting to make contact show the spirits that your motivation is correct by developing your spiritual self and reading lots of spiritual literature first. Become more aware of your inner being by turning off the outside world for a while and exploring and opening up your inner self. One of the best ways to do this is to become conscious of your breathing. Close your eyes and slowly breathe in and out. Each time you breathe out let go of negative thoughts and fears and as you breathe in feel the energy of light and love entering you. This energy is subtle and can only be sensed through your feelings.

Breathing exercises, like the one above, are simple meditations that can help you centre yourself and become aware of your inner being or voice. Every time you sit in silence and focus inwardly, or stop doing and simply be, something magical starts to happen; you begin to tune into cosmic energy and this in turn energises the creative spirit within and around you.

If sitting in absolute stillness isn't for you meditation

can be done in many ways. For example, you can get the same kind of focused energy when you dance, sing, act, paint, work, write, teach, inspire, lead, create and so on. Whenever you tune into the creative force within you and live fully in the present moment you are in fact meditating.

With patience, love and discipline and a growing awareness of your feelings you will start to become more spiritually aware. Don't be put off if you don't see results right away or if you don't find meditation easy. It can sometimes take time for spirit to awaken your energy but if you are patient and keep your mind and your heart open you will make progress.

You may at this stage decide to visit a medium or spiritualist church or you may find that spirits are letting you know they are around in ways that don't involve the use of a medium. In fact spirits of lost loved ones are forever trying to reassure us that they are there. There are various ways they try to do this and here are some of them:

- Music: Spirits can impress their energy on a song or piece of music so that you think about them when it is played.
- Psychometry: You may find that holding clothing or objects belonging to a lost loved one can trigger images, thoughts or feelings.
- Clocks: Clocks or watches may stop working for no obvious reason.

- Telephone: You may hear the phone ringing but when you pick it up no one is there.
- Electrical appliances: Radios, TVs and other electrical appliances may stop or start for no reason when no one is around them.
- Screens: Spirits have been known to scramble images on television or computer screens.
- Lights: You may notice that lights flicker or that new light bulbs burn out instantly.
- Smells: A common way spirits try to get our attentions is scent. You may suddenly become aware of the faint smell of a flower or cigar or familiar perfume and these scents are associated with people who have passed over.
- Animals: Sometimes spirit beings will influence a bird or animal to get our attention in some way.
- Silent shadows: Unexplained shadows glimpsed in the corner of the eye. You may also experience a feeling of being watched but when you turn around no one is there.
- Dreams: The spirit body leaves the physical body every night when we sleep. In the dream state we are able to see our loved ones and guides.
- Visions: For those who are very receptive and not mentally blocked it is possible to see visions of a lost loved one.
- Unexplained noises: Footsteps, knocks, banging, rapping, scratching sounds, sounds of something

being dropped. Sometimes these noises can be subtle and other times they can be quite loud.

- Doors, cabinets and cupboards opening and closing: Most often, these phenomena are not seen directly. For example, you return to find a door open you are sure you shut.
- Thoughts and feelings: Whenever you think about a lost loved one they are with you in spirit.
- Gust of wind: You may experience a draft, blast of fresh air or a breath of air on your face.

Spirits try to get our attention in many ways; you just need to start looking out for them. Whatever way you decide to approach the spirit world never forget that every time you call on a departed loved one with your thoughts and your heart they will hear you loud and clear.

THEY CAN HEAR YOU LOUD AND CLEAR

I can assure you that every time you think about a departed loved one they are with you. But remember that just as you have a life and work to do on earth they also have work to do spiritually. So if you keep obsessing about a lost loved one you will be preventing them from getting their important spiritual work done.

Obviously in the early stages you may find it impossible not to think constantly about a loved one who has passed over. This is perfectly natural as you need comfort and time to adjust to your new way of living and the spirit who has passed also needs your reassurance to help him or her adjust to a new life in spirit. But as time journeys forward the loving thing to do is to gently let the spirit of a departed loved one go. This doesn't mean you shouldn't think about them at all – that would be unthinkably wrong as it would cause both them and you pain – it just means don't think about them too much. Obsessing will not only hold them back but also stop you moving forward with the great and wonderful adventure that is your life.

Remember, the greatest, most powerful and most healing love of all is the love that can set a spirit free.

FEAR OF FLYING

Most of us find it hard to talk about death or to think about the prospect of our own death or the death of a loved one but from my experiences of the spirit world I want to leave you with the thought that death is not an end. It is just another stage in your existence. In fact you start dying the moment you are born and every night when you go to sleep your consciousness leaves your physical body and travels to the spirit world. When it re-enters your body in the morning it returns with dreams some of which you may understand and others you may not. In a sense it doesn't really matter whether you understand your dreams or not it just shows you that living and dying is happening every day of your life whether you realise it or not.

Sadly, our society has built the event of death into one of great fear and few of us are prepared for it. That's why it is vital that you grasp the idea that death is a beginning and that there is more in store for you and for loved ones you have lost. I hope this book has helped show you that there are many wonderful things that cannot be explained and that death is not something to be feared. Death is just another natural process and, in both this life and the next, it is guilt, fear, hate and anger that drag you down and courage, creativity, laughter and love that lift you up.

Living in spirit will not always be easy but never forget that you are not alone; your guides and departed loved ones in the spirit world will always be with you, however alone or lost you may feel. Try to open your mind and your heart to the possibilities of the spiritual aspects of your being and to think in the most positive ways so that you can help both yourself and those around you find their inner strength. By doing this you play your part in bringing spirit down to earth and when death finally visits you not only will you leave the world a better place you will be flying, without regret or fear, towards your new spiritual home, which some call heaven.